Trump Has
BLOWN IT!

by Maurice Hise

RoseDog Books
PITTSBURGH, PENNSYLVANIA 15238

RoseDog Books
585 Alpha Drive, Suite 103
Pittsburgh, PA 15238
Visit our website at *www.rosedogbookstore.com*

ISBN: 978-1-6495-7901-0
eISBN: 978-1-6495-7922-5

CONTENTS

CHAPTER 1
Trump Has Blown

TRUMP REALLY HAS BLOWN IN THE WHITE HOUSE. One of his first agendas was to tighten up the USA with immigration laws to build a wall to stop the crossing of illegal immigration. Donald Trump is like Clint Eastwood, who played in the movie *The Good, The Bad, and The Ugly*. At times Trump seems to be good and then he turns bad and his ways become very ugly. The way Trump has treated minorities by throwing them into the holding cells for deportation to escort them back to their countries, sometimes the parents become separated from their children while being obtained. Illegal immigrants that are working in the USA without a green card, you will be deported back to your country.

Donald Trump likes to shoot first and then ask questions later. The president is very quick to the draw when it comes to politics and running this country, just like his TV show, *The Apprentice*. Trump wants to fire you and embarrass you. Instruments are very different like the trumpet, the sound is different than the saxophone and a trombone. Trump's music is different, ear piercing to the mind, body, heart, and soul, his style is unorthodox, God Almighty will use the trumpet to sound off when he takes his Church home, you will hear the sound from miles away. Donald Trump is blowing his trumpet, powerful, a sound that is waking up the American people for change, the world is in a state of shock, in disarray. People's lives have been turned upside down for the better or the worse. American people have no sense of direction when dealing with Donald Trump. The president must have a golden spoon in his mouth. It seems that he was spoiled when he was a baby because when he can't get his way he becomes rude and obnoxious. He be-

1

comes very outspoken to the American people, there's no respect for liberty and freedom of life. American people want to know, has Trump been conducting business with Russia while going through his impeachment, to see if he has abused his power against the Constitution, as the American people found out Trump was not impeached. Is the president playing a deadly game of Russian Roulette with the United States? Trump is making his presence felt. Fighting for this great country with a different strategy, outspoken is his ways of methods. There is a new sound coming out of the White House, time for change for the American people.

Donald Trump is taking a stand against other countries to let them know to stay out of our airspace, land and our seas. Understand that Donald Trump is no pushover, he will fight for the American people at any cost, if that takes World War 3. Donald Trump is in the business of playing baseball, hard balls without a catcher, everything he throws is fast balls. It seems like the president only knows one speed to throw the whole kitchen sink at you without thinking first. Is the world heading for Armageddon War? Trump is putting his name in the history books, sooner or later it was going to be time for a different president, with a different agenda in the White House. The New World Order has been in place for decades in the foreign countries, because of dictatorship and leadership over people, the United States is next in line to rule the people with the Iron Fists, destruction is Upon Our Land how to set the pathway to try to clean the world up through a New World Order. Trump is gaining control over our land to clean up the system, stop immigrants from crossing over the border. The president is letting it be known if you do not have the right papers to come over here stay off of our soil, President Trump is gaining ground against the different nations that come to this land, with different beliefs than the American people trying to ruin our cultures and not following the guidelines in Liberty. Trump is Standing Tall in the White House, causing Havoc to the Supreme Court and firing Great and Mighty People that have stepped down from their positions because they did not believe in the president's system of thinking. Trump has gotten under a lot of people's skin, he will not allow the smuggling of illegal immigrants to come across this land. No more dirty trash will be tolerated Upon This Land, we have to live by the right standards as American people. No longer will you have an attitude saying that you can live over here illegally for free and not paying taxes. Whoever you are that's been in this land taking advantage of our system and our ways of right living.

When Donald Trump became president of the United States he was overwhelmed, fearful of his position. It's like being thrown into the bottom of the ocean blindfolded at nighttime. In a panic going off his instincts, swimming back to the top of the ocean, still blindfolded, waiting to see who will be by his side. Swimming back to shore can be very challenging, especially if people want to see you fail. The world will test you to see what you're made of, when they learn that you're not a pushover they begin to back up. Continue to show your strength and beliefs, never let them see you sweat. The president stays red a lot in his face because he is steadily blowing his trumpet. You have to really blow hard to make a sound beautiful to the ears if you know what you're doing. If you don't take time to practice or study the techniques in blowing breath control you sound terrible. Who wants to hear a bunch of noise, so far Trump has blown amazing. His sound is quite like no other, is it Heavenly or demonically, that is the true question, who is his true source to power, what side is he on, who is in his inner circle that he can truly trust, who is helping him make his decisions? A unit, a bond of trust, somebody that will take a stand to fight for what you believe in. Can we truly put our trust in the president, can we believe a word that comes out of his mouth? Does he really want to make this land great again to make this nation stronger?

Where is the true value of this great land? You must learn to adapt to the right standards of living through Almighty God . In God We Trust. Rest in God, don't worry about the president in the White House, whether he is right or wrong. God promotes who he wants to raise up and to put down. If we do our job in society and be honest everything will work itself out for the good, because we put our faith in God, not in the system. To be bullied doesn't feel good and this is what the world is experiencing since Trump has been in the White House, people are wondering will it stop, dealing with a racist president. All nationalities living in this great country feeling the backlash of a racist president, you're nothing but a number in a productive world, people are not treated as one. The USA picks and chooses different nationalities that they love and that they tolerate, as long as you are walking by their rules and standards, you will not become a Target. Prejudice, racism, mental hatred, the breaking down of a belief in a system of togetherness, now there is a balance on the playing field, you now have an understanding of the struggles black Americans go through just to have a piece of this land. Now you understand the oppression and depression, this might be a land of freedom of Liberty. Then why are minorities walking with shackles on their feet, we were all created by the same God of the universe. Foreigners living over here in the United States with a chip on your shoulder, saying the United States is weak, bringing Devastation to the land, your days are over. There is a new president in the White House and you can no longer sit back and reap off the land if you haven't put in your Blood, Sweat, and Tears into this country by illegally being over here.

Donald Trump is separating the wheat from the tares, people have become very frustrated while the president fights for rights standards. Trump is in the White House, the fire is starting to burn higher, is the fire supposed to be put out or to burn higher, it is very difficult to understand the degree of how the fire is burning, now you have become caught up in the smoke, which now has turned into combustible Heat, unable to put it out. The world is now on fire by Donald Trump, the hatred that you have for the president will continue to keep his fire burning. When President Trump got into the White House he was just starting to smoke through his thoughts and actions getting displayed. Now the roof is on fire, we don't need no water, let the nations burn, the bad infirmities across the land. When you see Donald Trump turning red a lot in his body, that's different degrees of Fire ready to come out of him at a rapid pace, cooking his enemies through the fire just like steak. Some people like their steak to be cooked well done, medium rare, or pink, whatever way it takes for Trump to cook your steak he will burn you with his fire. Trump is cooking upon the land, if you're doing wrong it's time to start booking because the fire is going to burn you, it's designed to cook a way, every day life struggles through sickness and disease, poverty, and homelessness, hate crimes, you name it. Let the Fire Burn. When you get ready to cook barbecue instructions on the bag for the charcoal, line them up in the pyramid position. When the charcoal turns white on the outside it's time to cook. Just like Trump, it takes time for him to cook but he's unpredictable, he might have the charcoal that doesn't need lighter fluid. You have to know what you're doing when you're cooking barbecue. You have to know when the Flames are too high or the charcoal's not hot enough, it takes a professional to know how to cook in the White House and to care for the American people. How many years do we taste Trump's BBQ, four years or 8 years?

CHAPTER 2
Speed Racer

IT SEEMS THAT EVERYTHING THAT THE PRESIDENT DOES IS IN ONE SPEED, he only knows one gear and that's the fast Lane, the president has a taste for Speed and we know the speed can be very dangerous when you're out of control. Just like life is out of control, breaking down barriers. We can be productive to better our economy as USA citizens. Trump is now starting to speed through the White House, a Need-for-Speed adrenaline junkie. Donald Trump is racing at a very high speed, sending a message to the foreign countries our nation is strong. We will no longer be in a deficit financially or physically or mentally or spiritually. Speed is very motivated to bring change to the USA. Donald Trump is showing his power. Mess with the bull, you get the horns. Speed Racer is showing the United States that we are not a weak country. Donald Trump is making sharp turns on the Runway, leaving his opponents in shock, bringing fear when you challenge him. Trump is making Maneuvers that we haven't seen before, they are very heartfelt. When the Smoke Clears from Donald Trump's tires you've been lost in the Wind, the start time has been very fast since he's been in the White House. His burst of speed is giving him the advantage to stay in the lead, to gain control over his opponent, to deal with Society, to understand the morals of our economy. Speed Racer drives muscle cars to keep him safe. When dealing with the Supreme Court, politicians, Democrats, foreign countries, the president's morals, the way he thinks, his head is very big, he doesn't need a helmet to cover it up, does the president wear seatbelts when he's racing or is he being Reckless and naïve? Does he truly understand that the American people are in his hands for safety and Trust? Sometimes his tactics are very abrasive and dangerous, it could become life threatening, it's like a deer caught in headlights, there's no way to Escape.

Donald Trump is motivated to take on any type of impact he faces, this is what his speed is designed for, it's very sufficient for him. Does it become Reckless at times because of the speed that he is going? Very effective against the enemy because they cannot keep up with his power, a Need for Speed and control, does this make him a Madman like Mad Max that Mel Gibson played in by stripping everything bare to the knuckle? Speed Racer is learning how to rebuild and build again in the USA. Define the right Solutions for everyday living. Trump doesn't care how dirty his cars are designed to be productive to get the job done. I would sure like to know who is keeping Donald Trump's cars clean, making sure that the car has everything running in good fashion, who's his mechanic? If Donald Trump has a second term in the White House you'll see him reach speeds that are unapproachable, he'll be Untouchable to his opponents. Trump will become a Lethal Weapon, bullheaded, hard to deal with, no remorse, unmovable, and stubborn in his ways. Nothing will be able to penetrate the skin, you already see the demeanor of Donald Trump, his hairstyle is explosive, it's like it has his own agenda. Speed Racer would use every bit of his political power to rebuild the structure of the United States. The president wants you to walk to his dictatorship, don't think for a second that he would not bring you down with him if that took World War 3, Speed Racer has become very sinister and none apologetic to the American people. He would blow the whistle in a minute for self-destruction if he thought he was being defeated. Trump is a radical president that is not scared to get his hands dirty. Thank you, God Almighty, for keeping your hands upon the United States.

Donald Trump will continue to keep his foot to the pedal to send a message to the foreign countries, the USA, it's our land of freedom of speech. Our land is no longer for sale, the country's over here with diplomatic immunity, you can no longer do what you want to do and piss on our soil. Stop showing off and talking about the American flag as you do business in our country, stop thinking that we are weak and pathetic and that anybody can trample over our ground. No more taking a dump on our land without toilet paper, but you tried to keep our land in a deficit of homelessness and poverty while your country is booming. We don't have to depend on foreign countries to generate revenues of money for the survival of our country, we have enough Firepower to make our economy big again with an industrial industry of the building of cars, production companies of clothes and shoes. President Trump is fighting for his country and he doesn't want to see not one American able to strive for equality for a landmark of success. Strategies and methods are plenty that Speed Racer can deal with against the enemy. Donald Trump has a lot of resources when it comes to the safety of the American citizens, remember the windtalkers. Our country is very dangerous because we have different nationalities living in this land, if we pull together as one unit, Unstoppable. Speed Racer must learn how to control his speed, at times it could be detrimental to the country. The president must have the knowledge to understand the movement of the car, while the American people are being moved in Society.

With the combination of all nationalities in the USA, Trump can use this to his advantage, to gain ground for the strengthening of the United States. With a master game plan we would defeat any opponent who comes to this land unannounced. Learn how to knock first to get the permission to come across our great land. It's time for all nationalities to learn how to share land and property, by pulling together we can make our economy the number-one capital of the world. To generate farming, agriculture, industrial plants, automobile factories, we have everything in place in this great country. Production is the key for the United States, that's why Trump has the blueprint for success. If you are not in the business of contributing to this great land, pack your bags and leave, to the different nationalities that are over here in the United States, you can no longer sit back, to live off the wealth of the American citizens. The United States has been good to you when you came over to this country, you were able to get $20,000 two 40,000-dollar loans to establish your business. We will not take for granted the Blood, Sweat, and Tears that our ancestors work so hard for to live in the United States. It's been a blessing to come over here and live with a different nationality, this country has let you in with open arms. So stop having hatred against the American people and flaunting your cultures like yours are more Superior than ours, there is a reason why you are over here in this great land, to live life freely and not to be dictated, so why dictate? America is so popular that every nationality wants to live in this great country because we specialize in togetherness.

CHAPTER 3
Hands of Time

The world is being pressure cooked, every time I turn around somebody's on TV talking about Donald Trump, how the economy is being affected, so he's not respecting the constitutional rights. People are talking about the business deals he's trying to set up with Russia. Donald Trump's Hollywood Walk of Fame has been vandalized three or four times. Frustrated because they did not want to see him have the recognition of anything. They have spray-painted the star and everything else. Trump loves to get a response from the American people, he doesn't care if you are offended by him, he has a job to do. Your hatred for Donald Trump is getting in the way of him trying to make this world a better place, believe it or not he has brought some justice to this world, the economy was just starting to grow until the Coronavirus, by the hatred that the American people are starting to display, the world is being divided through strife and unbelief. This is forming the New World Order, it has to take all nations and races to form this New World Order. Spread like a wildfire to the foreign countries, leaving America to turn into a dictator country. Through the violence in a rage in war, the system will collapse into World War 3, the Armageddon War. Everything has been set in place, concentration camps upon the land, Marshall law ready to go into effect. Manmade plagues that are upon the Earth. Coronavirus, splicing of DNA through foreign countries. Hands of time are upon us, a virus that has spread across the whole world, putting people in fear and doubt, to be in quarantine. What kind of madman would develop a plague to unleash it on his own people and watch it spread through the whole world?

Understanding the world collapses, big brother has his eyes everywhere where he can watch you at all times. Don't get caught up in the system of Technology, to the internet, cable, smartphone, you name it. I Robot is on the verge of taking over everything, it is already affected by civilization. Man wants to be replaced by machine, fiber optics. Everything is computerized, everything can be started by a push of a button, shut down by a push of a button. There's no freedom of privacy. The world is starting to live into bondage, caught up in the deadly cycle of life. It blows my mind just to think that man has gotten beside himself to create weapons of mass destruction, they can destroy the face of this Earth, it sounds like the New World Order, being American citizens we wage the war with freedom of speech, we have citizenship in the United States, not to be told what time to wake up or to go to sleep. We strive for equality, now the right to live free. United States citizens will not allow anybody to rule over us like an iron fist like the foreign countries do. Innocent civilians that are chained up like dogs starve to death because of a failing system. Information can travel at a speed of light, it can be put in your database in seconds, before you blink twice it is there for you to achieve. Organize your life. Put your trust in God, positive thoughts, Renewing Your Mind, understanding that life will work itself out for the better. Exercise releases stress and depression when you learn to shut down mood swings, anxiety attacks, bipolar schizophrenic thoughts, do not allow the cares of life to put you in a suicide mode, everything is spinning out of control, pray to God Almighty.

Now it's time to take a moment to look at your life whatever things you didn't do right, now it's time to fix them. Whether building right relationships with people, getting out of a life of poverty, going back to school to educate yourself to have a better life for your family. Understand your race and what makes you strive for equality. Learn how to live a productive life for your community, it's not where you come from but where you're at. You have been given a better opportunity than your parents to succeed in life, not being Afflicted through poverty, homelessness, abusive family, dealing with drugs and alcohol, mental and physical and verbal abuse, make sure that your bloodline is cleaned up, that you stop generational curses just running down the family tree, the little children have suffered enough in life society today. Civilization is important for the pivotal of our growth so that this nation will stand strong and be very productive. Trump is Now setting the stage to affect the economy for years to come. No direction in the White House, no Foundation or right formula to make this world successful. Donald Trump has been put in the White House to clean house, Supreme Court Democrats and politicians. Everybody is trying to fight for power to see who will back down as the world is in shackles. Donald Trump is the president, this is a true reality, so wake up out of your sleep, America, somebody does care about the welfare of this great nation, does the president of the United States believe if the economy starts to collapse the American people will start to move in fear and doubt, looking for a solution to ease the world out of pain? The dictatorship and Leadership that is not in the USA, people will be in financial problems having to depend on the government, will be the beginning of freedom of speech, Liberty to fight for our beliefs in this great land. Civilization in our manhood is being challenged by the government to move to a New World Order. It's going to take all the nations over here to fight as one, we must have a game plan of attack to fight for the right cause so the district Nations United States we will not be put in shackles in our minds. People must understand what they are fighting for, land, property, businesses. It's very important that you have the right legal documentation to fight to be in the United States. All nationalities combined together, we can take a stand against scrutiny, wrong Behavior patterns, to fall down to a New World Order, it's not the American people. The government has the right to seize all properties if you don't respond to their rules and regulations, just like the government with the census to see how many people are living in each house. Coronavirus breakout is designed for the New World Order to study the human race to see how people respond to dictatorship, sickness, and disease upon the land, homelessness and poverty. The whole world has been on shutdown concerning this virus that was manmade to see the strengths and weaknesses in people. I truly believe that this is going to start the resistance if people will wake up and understand how our lives are being affected on a day-to-day basis.

The USA has been lacking in a lot of situations when it comes to the welfare of the American people, dealing with foreign countries, learn how to say yes and no, don't let your dignity and pride rob the consumer. Demolition work starting to be done by President Trump, the USA needs a scrub down, a thorough cleaning. To rid the world of famine. Stop diplomatic immunity, confusing our system with bad business deals. It's time for our light to shine for the whole world to see if we have confidence in one another, we can see the light at the end of the tunnel. Time for rest, nothing but peace and tranquility. People have the right to express themselves. The hands of time are on the United States. People, don't hide no more, don't let people run over you, stop being bullied and harassed. The Good, the Bad, and the Ugly, we have seen now Donald Trump clean the world. Are we in right standing with the president? Remember, you voted him in, the things that the president does, is it business or personal, that's what's so hard to determine, one thing I do know is that he brings excitement to the game. We never become bored because he always has something up his sleeve, to keep us walking on eggshells at any time, we can crack in our minds, like putting on a blindfold and you can't see anything and we have to depend on the president to guide us through. It's a very dangerous thing that the president has the keys to our world. He can come into our lives anytime he wants to unannounced by force, let's pray to God that he doesn't abuse his power and Destroy humankind like Hitler. Trump seems to be troubled at times when I look at him on TV, but only God knows what he is holding in his soul. When Trump said that China knows what they did he didn't break, he kept his composure.

CHAPTER 4
Believer

IT IS TIME FOR EVERYBODY TO BE HELD ACCOUNTABLE FOR WHAT they believe in, does the world believe in God, we cannot deny that there is an all-powerful God that rules the universe. Signs of the time are everywhere, a world turned upside down and all around, the change of guard by Donald Trump being in the White House, we have to have faith, continue to pray to Almighty God , empowering of the Holy Spirit to protect us from danger seen and unseen. Donald Trump is the president, we need guidance from Almighty God . Pray that Donald Trump will bring the right balance to the USA through dignity and respect to understand the days that we are living in the Holy Spirit breaks chains and yolks, to keep Justice upon the land, God's security to keep us safe from devastation, from evil dictators forcing the New World Order in the USA, also foreign countries. Coronavirus, man-made, what's next, nuclear bombs, egotistical ways of man to destroy civilization? What is the Constitution built on, all people should be treated equally. So why is this separation and Division against the human race, we all bleed the same but don't believe in the same morals. *The Awakening* by Dr. Billye Brim, a powerful book movement of the forefathers throughout the land. Jonathan Edwards, George Winfield, Benjamin Franklin, black robe regiment, many more Great Men. To learn your history about the founders of this world, the movement of the Holy Spirit, you need to read this powerful book, to understand the faith that it took to build a backbone of success for the operation of the world. *The Awakening* by Dr. Billye Brim.

I was totally amazed when I read the book *The Awakening* by Dr. Billye Brim. I understood the moving of the Holy Spirit, back in the days people could not deny the movement of the Holy Spirit, just like these days. Dr. Billye Brim is a very powerful woman that has many books out. Strong, True Revelation in every book that she writes a gift from God. I was truly blessed to be in her presence when she came to our church, the anointing filled the church. What a powerful prophetess, she began to speak into people's lives, speak healing and deliverance. Stories that she told, it changed the face of American history. A deposit was installed into me through the Holy Spirit to write a part of *Trump Has Blown*. Dr. Billye Brim said when she was writing her book before the 2016 election, she said she knew Trump was going to be president. Supernatural Revelation was given to her friend Dr. Ben Carson, Trump would be president, June 2016. Dr. Ben Carson invited 1000 people to come to New York to pray about elections. Trump became president, Dr. Billye Brim said that there was a lot of tension through the churches because people did not believe in Trump's methods. His actions were very outspoken and malicious and defensive, to the American people. She went on to say that we have to understand the movement of the Holy Spirit, and not to get caught up into our emotional Realm. It's time to put our faith and trust in God, no matter what the president is displaying.

Dr. Billye Brim said that she would support Donald Trump. At first she did not believe in him until a revelation by God. People were shaking their heads in church what Dr. Billye Brim was speaking, she went off to say even though the things that Trump is doing, he needs to make better decisions. That's why we need to pray more for him instead of criticizing him. A hard pill for people to swallow. Dr. Billye Brim is an ambassador in the USA and foreign countries, people listen when she speaks. She has a strong reputation through TBN, her family is Kenneth Copeland, Benny Hinn, Mark Hankins. Foreign countries give her permission to speak on their soil and that is very rare. *The Awakening* the book talks about Lewis Island, Donald Trump's mother, the movement of the Holy Spirit, how it changed the island, Mary Anne MacLeod, the president's mother's name, she came from Northern Scotland, a remote island of the Brides better known as Lewis Island. People on the island had a one-on-one experience with the Holy Spirit. It was a Great Awakening from 1857 to 1859, went hand-in-hand, also a book *Wesley Duewel Revival Fire*, talks about the Ulster Awakening, everything we're together, the movement of the Holy Spirit. The Hebrides is a series of islands

40 miles west part of Northern Scotland, it said that Lewis Islands is also attached to one big Island about 60 miles long, back in the 1800s it was a population of 25,000 people that were touched by the Holy Spirit. Can we believe in something because Donald Trump's mother had the anointing of the Holy Spirit upon her life?

Before the Holy Spirit swept through Lewis' Island, the people were traditional in their truth and religion of belief, being strict in their ways the reverence of God, carnal actions. Before they ran face-to-face into the Holy Spirit. Please pick up the book, Dr. Billye Brim, first of all and *The Awakening* information comes from a book, *Sounds from Heaven, the Revival* on the isle of Lewis. Dr. Billye Brim did her research about Lewis Island 1949 to 1952, published in 2004. From 1930 Donald Trump's mother went on a hard fishing boat 7 hours, to reach the mainland. Scotland, that is before beginning a long Voyage over the Atlantic Ocean to get to America. The leading and guiding of the Holy Spirit, she was given a new chance to live her life. So Donald Trump is a president that believes in the movement of the Holy Spirit Trinity. Trump's household was raised up in the God Almighty. Dr. Billye Brim talks about in her book when Trump became president his hands were on two Bibles, one that Abraham Lincoln used when he took his oath as president and the other Bible his mother gave him when he graduated Sunday School, so you must understand the weight of the world that Donald Trump is feeling, on his shoulders. He has to keep his faith in God. He must renew his mind through the Holy Spirit, a gift that was imparted into him by his mother. Stop being so quick to point fingers at every little thing the president does. Trump will have to answer to God Almighty how he has been leading this nation, for freedom of opportunity, Liberty of Justice, freedom of speech, everybody treated equally. Impeachment for the president is not a solution, do we believe in the Constitution?

Life Must Go On, we now have a little background on Donald Trump and how his mother was very strong a woman of faith that was Guided by the Holy Spirit. Donald Trump was raised in a loving home where his mother taught him the word of God. The president knows the voice of God, he also knows when he's being disobedient and not listening to God, the president must not allow anger to get him off course, to put this information in this book was very important to me, so people would take another look at the president. There's two sides to a coin, don't judge a book by its cover. I would once again like to thank Dr. Billye Brim, her book first of all and *The Awakening*, forefathers Constitution fight for freedom, The Birth of a Nation. Declaration of Independence between the North and South, struggle for land and property to be American citizens. The great Jonathan Edwards, George Whitefield, George Washington, Benjamin Franklin, black robe regiment. I was really educated in reading the book. I came to the conclusion that some people do care about the welfare of this land, Trump does. I've also learned through Dr. Billye Brim that we can move forward instead of backwards, buy all nationalities and races treated equally so we all have room to learn. To the Pioneers that suffered and died on this great land, God bless you. To the nationalities that were brought over here, you have a voice platform, use it to your ability. Don't let hatred and Prejudice keep corrupting our soil, pull together as one, this world would be a much safer and better place.

CHAPTER 5
Wake Up

THERE HAS BEEN A LOT OF PROTESTING GOING ON IN DIFFERENT cities and states, people protesting against Donald Trump. The time clock cannot be turned back, now that Trump is president, we must move forward and accept our responsibilities for voting Trump in. Why are people protesting because of discrimination, racial violence, color of your skin. All Nations need to pray and Stand for each other. If you are over here illegally, you have no right of freedom of speech. God Almighty has put Trump in the White House, no matter if you believe in the president or not. As the world has been hit with the Coronavirus, we see the president fighting for the American people, together we will triumph over this disease.

Now is the time to clean the USA up after we've gotten through the Coronavirus. If you're living over here and you're not hiding anything, there's no need to sweat about the politics. People of power in the White House, the Supreme Court, you name it, no longer lie, steal, cheat, against the American people for political gain to play games with civilian lives. Man has no right to dictate freedom of living, we need a system that is pure, righteous, clean, and holy. Legal documentation must be shown if you come from a foreign country to live here. A lot of people that snuck over here to this great land, it's time to answer for your actions, especially the ones bringing landmines of Destruction to our soil. Don't get scared now because your time has come, you played long enough in this land, everything must have an ending, judgment has come upon the Earth, God Almighty is doing a census, so is the government, the illegal immigration, in the USA is off the charts definitely in the Millions. No longer will the government be caught sleeping, while taking post, Donald Trump will see to that.

Emotions can no longer stand in the way because of the system, flexing their muscles whether they're right or wrong. Embrace change, it's here, this world is being turned upside down, everybody's going through changes because of President Trump. If you are an upright citizen things will work itself out. God has put a system in effect that will change the world, take life second by second, minute by minute, hour by hour. Patience is the key, you cannot Rush the hands of time, there had to be a shaking in an Awakening for the American people. Time to make adjustments, everyday living can become an overload if you let it. Take your eyes off the tactics that Trump uses and look for change to our economy. If you do good you will be rewarded for good, if you do bad you will be rewarded for bad. Does the dollar bill say "In God We Trust," not man? Right now the train is going very fast, now that Trump is president. The Coronavirus slowed everything down, people have been asked to shut themselves in, everyday life is at a standstill right now, people are in shock, total disarray, unbelief, scared, confused. Don't let fear keep you in bondage, All Nations and races, now's the time to pray to God Almighty.

Because of the chain of events protesting has died down, because of the Coronavirus the world is on lockdown, a lot of people were protesting for the wrong reasons, wrong motives. Direction is the key, protesting means you have evidence to be secure, you must have a reason to agree or disagree information to get your point across. Words can be damaging or uplifting, research is important. Never be put in a situation where you're uncomfortable, always have the right details. Liberty is very important, everybody's voice makes a difference. Take time to listen to the Next Generation, stop ignoring the teenage, the children. Protesting for change in our environment is crucial, right standards of living. Since the world has been slowed down by the Coronavirus, everybody's on the same playing field to defeat this enemy together. Protest to stay home, get the word out, epidemic will not last long if we do our part. As I write this book I don't know how long the Coronavirus will last.

The world has time to stay home, it's important that parents raise their children together, fighting in the family, bringing emotional damage to the children. Spend time with your children so they would not become isolated. The children are ignored, they feel they have no voice to express themselves.

Single parents raising up their children, no balance in the household. Children become dysfunctional, go to the streets looking for peace of mind, become involved in gangs, drugs, stealing, Menace to Society. Girls become pregnant, confused in their minds, Lose self morals. Families must pray together, children will not fall victim to Life Society, children are pictures to our environment, stop neglect, abuse. Children are being mistreated all throughout the world, abandoned, no voice to speak, raised up in the wrong atmosphere. It's very important that households have the right balance, father and mother together, but that's not Society. Single parents, continue to strive hard for your children, you both will be rewarded. Next Generation, let's be prepared for success, not to see our children behind bars, land of opportunity, the USA, parents, let's make a difference through these hard times. Coronavirus should bring families closer together, not farther apart. Understand to have an innocent life in your hands, great responsibility raising children, both parents in the household, your fruit will prosper by Leading The Way.

We must take a stand day in and day out, things we deal with in families, houses are in shambles, family members, alcoholics, dope addicts, child abusers. Families deal with children being raped, not enough food or clothes or shoes. A life of arrogance, Pride, stubbornness, hatred destroys lives. Boys and girls need a functional family, not dysfunctional. Substance abuse destroys families, no reality to Everyday Life. It's stealing manhood and Womanhood, from your children, they carry the scars on their backs, how they have been hurt through life Society. Children do not need to be in prison in their minds, growing up in the households, while the parents self-destruct in front of their eyes, trials and tribulations. Dignity, don't let anything destroy your family, fight for what is right. Fathers and mothers, go home, your family needs you to clean yourself up. Install education to your children, to have a successful career. Fight positive, not negative, destroy generational curses, be held accountable for your actions. There's always a chance for recovery, don't throw in the towel however long it takes. Next Generation needs us to live a life of freedom, not bondage. After we get through the Coronavirus, the economy is going to be stronger like never before. What a crucial time in history for everybody to pull together, to become one. It's important to educate your children about things that would destroy their bodies, dear life. No one wants to see their children inflicted, buy drugs or poverty. We want to remember our children, precious babies turn into responsible adults.

The Coronavirus is a manmade tool, decade of years through hatred, prejudice, Pride, arrogance, violence, the virus experimentation, genetics splicing strands of DNA, spiritual entity unseen, operating to the physical. The disease lives of fear and unbelief. Thinking it would not be beat, Bringing death turmoil to the world. We have the power to defeat this virus if we all pull together. Once again man brought disaster to this world, it came from China, did the government know about this before it was Unleashed on people? Is this the start of the New World Order, to mess with the elections for November, to do a census, study of the humans Following instructions? To know how to force martial law when the time comes, to see how the economy will collapse, bring about the New World Order 666, the Number of the Beast. Dictatorship and Leadership keep the world in poverty and homelessness. God Almighty is watching to see who will pray for forgiveness, to stop the Coronavirus. I put this in the book for a reminder to remember where we came from and where we are at, trying times, I know, God forbid, when this book is out Coronavirus is gone. Don't let the system fool you, man is evil, God is the only one that can save us. You have to understand 2020 is a new decade. Everything is new for the better or the worse, be prepared for change. Trials and tribulations is just the beginning, everybody has learned something from this ordeal. Put your trust in God Almighty.

CHAPTER 6
Truth Hurts

I KNOW THAT EVERY FOREIGNER LIVING IN THE USA WOULD LIKE TO bring their families over here. That is not possible, unfortunately you cannot help everybody, count your blessings that foreigners are over here now. You came to the United States, depression, oppression, bigotry and dictatorship ruled you, so you had to get away from foreign countries destroying lives. Ungodly methods, torture, mind, Body, heart, soul, a system of bigotry, government worship, rule with an iron fist for the different nationalities that are over here in this great land. You carry the scars on your back, mind, you escape to the USA for freedom, but don't come over here with a chip on your shoulder, with jealousy working against the system, be equal as one, don't be envious of the way we live, embrace opportunities. You are making a difference is the USA, if we call you Americans, dream big, resources are part of the land.

Everybody Must understand their culture, nationality, history and generation. At some point in life you must understand who you are, you need to learn about your ancestors, what they stood for. How did they see life through their eyes, spirituality and religion? You need to understand the direction that you are going in Pathways that your family set up. Society is much better when you have an understanding in life. Doors will be opened up to you that your ancestors paved. Stories have been handed down from generation to generation, about the family trees. Countries got into exile, corruption, countries came into power. Third-world countries ,countries of War, famine. Important to understand your country's nationality, the forefathers and foremothers, you need to know what their rights were, through their leadership. A lot of foreign countries have fallen because of the dictatorship and Leadership of man, before the countries came into power, or countries that had no power, the library is a good source, read up on your history. You would be surprised by your ancestors, how some of them have turned the world into corruption, clearly not understanding that the next Generations had to live down here on this Earth. Why should they be held accountable for the mistakes that our forefathers and mothers have made?

Because of the mistakes the people have made by putting people into office to lead the way for a nation, millions affected evil dictators in government offices. People have been taken for granted. No Remorse, no respect. Foreign countries boys are taken from their families to be soldiers where they are ruled. They never have a chance to live as boys, teenagers. Their whole life is destroyed because all they know is war, to fight at age eight and up. Girls taken from their homes where they do not want to be married into families. Little girl sold to sex trafficking like a piece of meat, this is torture to the mind, body, heart, and soul. A lot of Filth and hurt going on in foreign countries, because of the dictatorship. Don't get me wrong, the USA has issues also. How can children be missing and abused and homeless, no food or shelter, there's a lot of plates that need to be cleaned Through The Souls of the people. My heart is broken when I hear about Children of the land damaged and hurt, they did not ask to come into this world, we all will be held accountable how we treat the children. We can all pick our game up to make this land more better productive. In order to have success you must work hard at it, it takes time.

It's been a lot of talk about the American consumers, workers are lazy, compared to the work ethic in the foreign countries. It is believed that they know how to work harder than Americans. Their production is way Superior than ours, we have no backbone or grit to work, automobile factories are connected with people overseas, higher revenue of sales, better product, state-of-the-art facilities, production 24/7. It has also been said in order to keep production going people in foreign countries are being overworked. Working 13 to 16 hours a day. It's all about the quota, they couldn't care less about the wear and tear on humans. That type of behavior will not be tolerated in the USA. A chokehold has been put on the economy since the Coronavirus. Trump is fighting harder to bring back civilization to the USA, the work field will become stronger than ever before, it will be more jobs for the American people, minimum wage will go up, everything has been turned upside down before the Coronavirus, Donald Trump wanted to see what the world was really made of, a lot of businesses and companies have been taking advantage of the American people, being overcharged by their product, Making it hard on the consumer while businesses are gaining extra profits.

Trump is putting his foot down on illegal immigrants in the land illegally, working for free, getting paid underneath the table, not filing W-2 forms. Trump has really started to crack down on immigrants that do not have their green card. Go through the right Channel to have the right documents to live in the USA. Trump has brought change to slow down the system, illegal Crossing. Immigrants have been coming over the Border for centuries and not following the rules, it's going to be harder to try to have residents in the USA now. I know a guy that met a Chinese girl on the computer, she wants to live in the USA so they got married with a green card, she had her credentials, as the years have passed they have found out that they don't love each other. A big house with 3 bedrooms and 2-car garage, sleeping in different rooms. Her green card is about to expire, she's having problems trying to get reinstated. Infidelity, affairs with different people, everything is a big mess right now, I'm quite sure there are millions of cases in the USA with people dealing with green cards. Since Donald Trump has been in the White House people have become scared and frightened, you can no longer hide over here in this great land. If you can't follow the rules and regulations, Sorry, you can't live here. Everything must come to an end if it is not legit. Never take anything for granted, especially if it's wrong, buy illegally, being over here in the United States.

How is our relationship with dealing with foreign countries telling them come over here with diplomatic immunity? Foreigners are squeezing their way right through the system. Is it affecting our Market with the right business trades, to make the United States successful? The United States can be successful without depending on foreign countries, they have too much leeway in our land, they don't respect the morals of our land, are they a threat to the economy? Foreign countries like China own parts of our land, so do other countries, can we buy back our land? Why should they have Deeds to the land? Diplomatic immunity is a disgrace. Does Russia or China have the right to fly over our Air Zone, do they have the right to test missiles over our sectors? Stop roaming over our oceans with your ships. No foreign country should have the right to hold American citizens captive to treat them to keep her mouth shut, the President says we need to have a game plan, a secret mission of attack. In order to deal with ISIS or any terrorist, we can no longer give away our strategies over the TVs. Stop putting information in newspapers, social media and the internet. Stop giving the enemy heads-up, it's very important to know who comes to our soil, so they cannot bring hate crimes. We will not stand for destructive Behavior, you will be held accountable for your actions. No terrorist ever again polluting our great land.

A little history about the Illuminati the forefathers of the USA started Journeys decades ago, setting up the structure of the USA, how they believe the country should stand for equal rights, to make sure the American people have the right Justice. Disagreement in areas with the government, dealing with war and politics in the economy, so the colony was born Illuminati, sparked a revolution, different sides were taking the splitting up of a government because they couldn't come to the same conclusion. Beliefs were different in making The USA strong. The government had their way of thinking, Illuminati had their way of thinking. Is Illuminati the muscle behind a lot of presidents like Trump, George W. Bush and his son, even Obama, they do exist, Freedom Fighters, whatever way you want to look at that. They will take a stand for this great nation against ISIS, any terrorist of hatred, whoever tries to get into their way will be brought down. Everything is for a reason, the good and the bad, God help this nation, whatever it takes for the security and Welfare of this great land. Illuminati will not stand for people who do hate crimes against the American people. If you're plotting and planning in the USA get out now. Everything is in shambles right now the way the borders have been opened up, foreign countries coming over and leaving this country. The government has not been able to keep track over everybody traveling from country to country. This is how the Coronavirus disease spread. Politicians, Democrats are crooked, extorting, and transferring our hard-earned money to foreign countries, making them rich, stealing from the American people, people of power in the White House, Supreme Court, you name it, are a bunch of Thieves, not everybody in the

White House, but I bet you a large majority of them are. The power of man wanting to dictate. This formed the Illuminati whether their beliefs are right or wrong, they have to answer to God Almighty. But to have protection in the USA we can sleep a little bit better. Illuminati was formed in World War I and got a true identity in World War II, people have left the government to follow them. Army, Navy, Marines, Air Force, Coast Guard, also Navy Seals, Special Forces, chemists, environmentalists, doctors.

CHAPTER 7
Let Down

THE WHOLE WORLD IS IN HIDING, A SENSITIVE WORLD, trust issues are now out the door, it's hard to believe in the system of the government, and law enforcement, a takeover of wrong motives has been put into our minds, hearts, and souls. Separation is really throughout the land, people do not know which way to turn, security has been beefed up because of Isis. The land we build, we have become prisoners to our own system. Trump is in the White House, can we trust the government, can Trump have faith in the Supreme Court? It's hard to understand Trump at times, especially when he degrades the women, does the president seem to be prejudiced or angry? He likes to confront people and tell them off, he will challenge you. Very rude and obnoxious and challenging, people need to be held accountable for their ways, in the White House, family businesses have been damaged because of the government rules. Faith to believe in the system, IRS, it's taxing businesses for every little thing. Trump has exposed the government, people are being very careless and Reckless, where is the American people's money really going to, foreign countries. Is there any liability in stocks and bonds? In order to rent out a building for your business can be high, you can't keep up with the payments, especially to rent a building downtown, you better know your business is going to be successful. The government is charging you all this money but then they have abandoned buildings sitting where nobody's being charged for the occupancy.

Donald Trump may not have the experience for the White House, he shows a lot of heart and dignity. Everything is being challenged to the White House because of the president. He's learning experience through Hands-

On, a threat in the office. Trump is getting everybody's attention, foreign countries also. People are quick to point the finger against Trump, he's not paying taxes. President Trump should pay for the wall to stop the illegalization, crossing over the Border. It seems to me that Trump is getting the job done whether you like it or not. A word spoken by somebody that is very strong sometimes brings on good results. Trump is the man in the White House, he won against Hillary Clinton. The things that Hillary Clinton was accused of didn't stop her chances of being president, some people said she would not have enough strength to be president. Would a woman get the same respect as a man, especially being president? Did Hillary Clinton waste millions of dollars dealing with foreign countries, helping immigrants, making bad business deals, sowing into Badland, American people that work hard for their money, nobody should have the right to swindle it away. Some of the things that Donald Trump has talked about people in the White House abusing their power, stealing money, people in the Senate, congressmen making wrong decisions to hurt our economy. Foreign countries do not want to see the United States healthy and prosperous.

It's very clear to see if the American people chose a man instead of a woman president, did you want the hardness of a man, or softness of a woman? No way in fashion or form am I putting a woman down, by playing baseball you need a hard ball. No softball. When Things become hard we need a man that can stand up to have faith to believe. We need somebody that can stay motivated, never throw in the towel, the Unshakable. Not to say that a woman is not capable or inadequate to be president, not this time around. In order to hold a great mantle you have to come to the game with a chip on your shoulder. What I mean by that is you have to be determined to know you will always win. Sensitivity plays no part in being president. You came into the game not worrying if somebody likes you or not, don't show sadness or to be vulnerable. Sometimes it takes for you to be on the island lost by yourself, find your way home. Everything cannot be a dream but reality. You have a responsibility to feed your sheep, to talk to them and care for them. Make them feel they can trust you, not alone. Finding a product you want if you're not convinced you won't buy it. President Trump had the sales pitch out of this world. People bought into it.

CHAPTER 8
Man and Woman

GOD CREATED MAN TO BE THE HEAD AND NOT THE TAIL. God gave man creation of everything, all the animals, you name it, God created Adam first and then Eve. God has made Man In His Image, God's DNA is in man, which has to have faith to move mountains, to make right decisions in life. Man was put down on the earth first. To cultivate the land and know how to work the land. Man has been given wisdom and knowledge, to handle anything that comes his way. Man has been made different than woman to handle pressure. Man was built to handle the emotional to Life's ups and downs. Wisdom and knowledge has been implanted into man to handle anything that comes his way. God said in his word women are the weaker vessels. So women were not built to handle a lot of turmoil, everyday life survivals. Man's job is to keep the balance between him and the woman. To make sure that she is not oppressed and depressed in everyday living. It is the man's job to release stress and pressure away from the woman. Man is the backbone to stay strong through any crisis, protector for his wife and family.

Man's job is to be stable and strong to keep stress off his wife so she can live a productive life, man and woman must learn how to become one, the woman's job is to pray for the man to stand in the gap for her man, to believe in him, to encourage him to keep the faith. Love him no matter what they go through to develop a bond. To trust each other is very important in a relationship, a woman must keep her man lifted up. Structure is very important for a man to keep stable, because if he falls the woman would be next. Belief and Trust in one another is the right key to healthy relationships. To become compatible in a relationship communication is the key. Sometimes all it takes is to say I'm sorry, don't let pride and arrogance get in the way. Would a woman be able to handle pressure of everyday life living as president? Would she be strong enough to interact with foreign countries, scared to say yes or no? Would she have the power to keep her foot on the pedal, bringing danger to the American people? Can she deal with the heavy weight on her shoulders, for the American people? Yes, women are very powerful and wonderful, is there always a chance that the woman still could faint, in the middle of controversy? Some of the things American people were thinking about when Hillary was running for president.

God said that is not good for man to be alone, that's why he created woman, but would it be fair to say that women should not be alone either? We have a lot of single parents raising children with no father in the home. No balance. The fathers are gone in the Wind, never to return home. The wear and tear against the mind, becomes very stressful. Her emotional Rim is attacked, she becomes physically and spiritually weak. Something that a single parent deals with. I take my hat off to single parents, the mother and father. With God you are never alone, your struggles belong to him. To the single parents, God will always have a ram in the bush for you, never be scared to get help from the government if you need it, there's nothing wrong with getting help to get on your feet. Single parents, you will be rewarded for your sacrifice and raising up your kids the right way.

Trump has an obligation to get the USA out of deficit, with foreign countries, no longer will our land be stepped on or mistreated. USA, land of freedom and opportunities. Do not be over here in the USA bringing destructions of traps, for the enemy to destroy our land. You have no right to live here, get out now, the president has the right to have all eyes on the whole world. It's time to keep monitoring the world, if you don't have anything to hide you're fine, but if you are hiding or planning something, your deeds will be exposed. Brothers keeping a tight lid over the USA, big brothers. Playing around is over, too much movement going on in our country. People are not being studied, who's going in and out. City, country, foreign countries. The government needs to understand the nationalities that are living in the USA. We do not need anybody from foreign countries bringing over blueprints of disasters, by teaching foreigners that live over here or anybody that does hate crimes, to try and plan destruction, like planting bombs in buildings, cars or on yourself. About time our borders are being secured. Trump will go down in history as a president that was Radical, that shocked the world. Cut From a Different Cloth, giving the American people a run for their money.

Over the decades there's been so many nations and races, they came to the USA for freedom. Over here in this great nation nationalities have raised kids from generation to generation. So we do not know if we're Sleeping with the Enemy or not. Could there be a plot that Isis is trying to recruit soldiers on our land? It's very important to monitor the world, any means necessary. The White House, Supreme Court politicians, the Democrats at war with each other, instead of agreeing together, putting down stricter laws who can travel to this great land. Who allowed our country to be infiltrated during 9/11, airplane strikes against our country should have been stopped. Could there be a World War III on the horizon? Armageddon War, blood up to a horse's bridle. Destruction of man to rule by any means necessary. Innocent blood was sacrificed in World War I and World War II. Because the struggle of power between different countries, if Uncle Sam wants you for war and you did not want to go you would be locked up, the government has the right to draft who he wants for war, teenager stages and adult stages. Young and healthy men and women ready to die for the country. No matter how you feel about the situation, you're just a number ready to be used, dictatorship and Leadership.

It's clearly to see that love is what's missing in the world, replace hatred with love. Hatred is a tool for Destruction. It destroys many lives. Do we understand the hatred that Donald Trump displays at times? Disgusted with the nation that needs to be cleaned up. All races with different faces in the USA, everybody held accountable. What caused the hatred in Trump, being a kid or teenager or an adult, was he rejected? Is it that he didn't get the attention that he was looking for? Now that he is the president of the United States, he's getting all the attention that he needs, showing true signs of obnoxiousness, cold hearted and calculating. It's very important to understand how people have been raised or what they have been exposed to. If Trump does not get his way, does he act like a big baby, and throw temper tantrums? The president is still learning how to show restraints of positivity and not negativity. Was he able to handle pressure when he was a teenager, we all know about peer pressure. We all need to take a deep breath and step back and think before we speak because our actions could be detrimental. Trump needs to understand making the right decisions can be a matter of life and death. He must not lead American people to the slaughter without reasoning and thinking, about the direction this world is going in, being president of the United States is not a game, something you can turn on and turn off. Prayer, patience, true diligence is required to Lead the American people, regardless if you like them or not.

The things that Donald Trump is doing may not seem pretty but effective. It's no longer time to sugarcoat the USA, dealing with the economy. Donald Trump is starting to gain traction, plowing through obstacles this world is facing, the president is making the blueprint that we won't run out of money by 2030. Turning into a poverty-stricken land, children have nowhere to lay their heads. Is the United States having financial problems with different countries? China and other countries with diplomatic immunity, robbing our system of living. Trump is climbing up the hill with momentum, setting a tone to see what countries are for us or against us. I know that a lot of people are distraught because Trump is president, the world would argue and say that God did not make him president, I hate to bust your bubble, yes he did, my emotions tried to get in the way while I was writing this book how I felt about Donald Trump. I stopped listening to the world and accepted my thoughts and not jumping on the bandwagon like other people. I had to have patience and sit back and watch this thing start to unravel, elections will be coming up November 2020. Trump has been a very productive president, it seems to me he has used his time wisely. The times that we are living in are very evil, Coronavirus manmade, we have to put our trust in God Almighty. So if you are mad at God Almighty, by putting Trump in the White House, you cannot tell the Potter how to bend the clay.

CHAPTER 9
Fight Weakness

IT'S TIME FOR THE WORLD TO RESIST, if you resist Satan he will flee from you. The world has been resisting Donald Trump because he has abused his power, but what is the definition of abusing power, the president was not impeached. Donald Trump walks to his own tune, do you think he was sweating when he was being impeached? He is very radical, especially when he resists against the American people. Resist me to put up a challenge or fight until things go your way. We all have to learn how to resist things, whether good or bad, Trump is a strong brick wall, if you let him rattle your mind, he will affect every fiber of your being. His ways are very repetitious, malicious at times, designed to keep you over the edge. White House has been exposed since Trump has been in office. Republican or Democratic Supreme Court light is shining on you, Trump truly wants to solve the problems of the USA, the whole world is in shock. Will the world be a better place since Trump is in the White House, is he a pushover? What type of power does he have that one man can shake up a whole world, where Trump stays on their minds?

We can all agree it is very scary when Trump puts his mind in action, resist against poverty, homelessness, drugs, violence, dictatorship. Let's fight and resist against generational curses, or the pattern of war that so easily takes us down, stop the cycle of war that has destroyed our loved ones. We must resist against mass destruction, New World Order. Man cannot have his cake and eat it too, why does jealousy and pride and arrogance always stay on the mind, no man or woman should say that they are better than one another. We all have a piece of the puzzle to play with if we understand the game. What is the game, to live equally as one, to Get along with each other.

We have to understand that there are bad substances out there, that lead to bad morals in life. Resist alcohol, crystal meth, cocaine, uppers and downers, heroin, anything that destroys the body family and life. Do not let the spirits keep you in bondage, you're traveling down the wrong path if you have to, steal, cheat.

We have to learn how to fight our weaknesses because the children are being affected. When fathers and mothers become selfish, cold hearted towards their children, they suffer. If you would do a census in the world, you will see how many abandoned children are out in the world today, there's a responsibility to be productive in your household. The children must have food, shelter, and clothing, a good education, understand the structure of raising children, understand your gross income that you make every year. It's very important that you learn how to budget your money, learn how to have money in the bank. It's time to learn true reality, if you had a baby in a year and then turn around and had another baby in a year, knowing that you're not financially set, you're making a big mistake. You find yourself living from paycheck to paycheck, especially when you're dealing with substance abuse. Fight weakness, now you're living off the system general assistance, which is nothing wrong with it until you can get on your feet, but if you have become lazy and depending on the system to take care of you, greed is taking over your family. Don't make the children suffer because of your Problems. Now you're having a breakdown physically, mentally and spiritually, you're in the business of looking for free handouts instead of finding a way to get off the system. Going back to school for a trade or working two jobs, whatever it takes to support your family at the highest level.

Do you know how many children are waiting to be adopted because of the mistakes of the parents, the children go from shelter to shelter, which is putting a ripple effect in their minds. They feel left and alone, that nobody wants them. When they become older they want to know where their biological parents are. If they find a home they have a lot of baggage on them from the trials and tribulations. Going through a system where they have not found a true identity. Scarred for life because they never find a true calling in life. So a lot of children Rebel, end up right back in the system because they are very hard to deal with. They do not understand Authority, can't get along with their foster parents. Some cases have been to the children being taken away from their parents because of child abuse or parents, drug addicts. We all must be responsible for our children, please stop neglecting the children. Report anybody that is abusing the children, no one should suffer. God Almighty loves the children, he will intercede for anybody that is being treated wrong. Stop making precious children that you can't take care of. Don't be quick to lay down, the quicker to give the baby away or abort the baby. The world should be tired of seeing 13-, 14-, 15-, 16-year-olds having babies, destroying their own lives.

CHAPTER 10
End Game

END GAME IS TIME TO MAKE A SACRIFICE TO BE A PRODUCTIVE CITIZEN in the United States. We must now strive for Liberty, everything is setting itself up for self-destruction. Is there an end game to civilization for no more happiness on this Earth? I'm talking about the chokehold on this Earth, to destroy the souls of humankind. A dictatorship of forcing the New World Order, a chain of command decided to affect the whole world. A one-world system where money will become extinct, credit cards with chips will be the new thing. Some places will not let you pay rent through a money order, you have to go online and pay, restaurants no longer want you to use a time card to punch in, they want you to put your thumb on a computer so they can scan it. It is now starting to become a part of people's businesses. Technology like this will track your information down in seconds and minutes, the growth and success of this world is always elevating itself. Everything is now becoming computerized. Is this a good thing or a bad thing, instead of having the old-school way with paper on file, computers are taking over. We have seen over the years that computers do break down, erasing all your important information.

Online seems to be the way keeping track of finances, checking and savings accounts, designed to know where you're at all times, keeping track of your jail or prison time or looking at your history. We're heading for a New World Order, time is moving very quickly. The world is facing a head-on collision, Americans don't know who to believe in. Everybody's trying to figure out where to turn to equal justice. We're dealing with a system that is failing, it wants us to be robots. It's time to establish your thinking to build walls, trust in God Almighty, pulling down strongholds of a failing system, our economy needs to be stronger so that we feel we have made a difference in life. Society in life is starting to wear the American people down, it shouldn't be Poverty or homeless throughout the world. Pressure is starting to build up on the minds and hearts of The Souls of the people, business and companies are laying off a lot of people, why not enough communication in the work field? People not pulling together with the right structures and business deals. Consumers not playing Fair, people not getting paid for what they really are worth. I don't have all the answers to the question but a piece of the puzzle, if everybody will use the piece of the puzzle that they've been given we could all have a better piece of life.

There's always going to be companies and businesses that don't believe in you, just like you have doubts about the system, does it really work? What does the word doubt mean, you are to be judged to decide between two or more choices to make a decision to separate into component elements or fact that you're in your decision to evaluate it carefully. A sense of hesitating to division in making a decision by waving back and forth. Understanding how to distinguish the two, not to be confused in your mind, without studying information, or not ready to face life's true reality. Sometimes life can bring on fear, especially when you hear about the New World Order, sometimes you wish that it was all a dream as we see what everyday life brings us. Is there a life's button that you can turn off and on dealing with Life Society, being faced with trials and tribulations every day you wish you could fly away to the sky. I know that change is a part of life, just like with President Trump, is it fiction or nonfiction, is he real or fake? Does he want the world to really be a better place, or does he want to really keep the world trapped in bondage, to make sure the economy is growing or to make sure it's suffering. Right now dealing with the Coronavirus, the world is suffering, did the president know about the virus ahead of time? Could he have slowed down the spread ahead of time or did he want to see the American people suffer together? Who knows, that doesn't seem like his makeup to me.

You must get a grip on your emotions, don't let the benefactors of Life bring you down. One minute you're up, the next minute you're down, that's no way to live life. There is a solution to the madness, you must have a balance to be productive. Put your trust in God Almighty, he will lead you, if you put your trust in anything else, man, wood, stones, drugs, alcohol, it becomes an idol that's taking the place of God, if you don't get your house in order, you will find yourself spinning and spinning, not able to grasp true reality. We all need a piece of mind when we go through life struggles. There's no way that you can get closer to God if you are arrogant and prideful. You must have a made-up mind to change, it's your responsibility, remember we are nothing but Dust in the Wind. We all have a voice, speak up, don't let the world tell you that it doesn't make a difference, it does, learn how to keep your emotions in check, if this world does not wake you up right now you have really been lost to society and things will not get better until you respond to change. Don't put all the pressure on Trump and point fingers, we all have been part of the solution, no, it's going to take a joint effort to pull together as one.

We have to give ourselves a chance to believe that the system will work itself out. Resist the theory of Doom and Gloom, understand that we are winners. Pray For Change against the Supreme Court, the Republicans and the Democrats, some become equal as one in order for the world to run smoothly. Dealing with mental attacks can bring on anger, mood swings, and rage, anybody dealing with symptoms should be prayed for. It's very important to pray for Donald Trump, so that he won't be led by the powers of Darkness when conducting business. Sometimes if he's put in an awkward position and he feels threatened, his behavior is not normal. Did the former presidents in the White House pray to the bones of their forefathers? It has been rumored that they did. Don't tell me the White House is in a cult, are they into witchcraft? People have been brainwashed for many years to become violent and destructive. Darkness always wants to take over the light to destroy the human race.

People that deal with schizophrenic bipolar, attacks in the mind, kill and destroy, it's a worldwide epidemic. Foreign countries deal with a lot of presidents that are very dictating. It seems like they are under the influence of the enemy, Demon possessed. A lot of families have suffered from foreign countries, they have lost everything, while the government is living it up. Understand it's a spiritual world we live in, not a physical one, no human being on this face of the Earth should have to suffer by the power of Darkness. The world has been through enough turmoil, especially right now with the Coronavirus. I thank God that the Coronavirus is on his way out, Trump has said that some states are ready to open up businesses again. I had to put this in the book to let you know where the state of the world is in right now, thank God for his mercy and his grace, if you have not learned anything from this ordeal you truly need a true reality check. My mind is more at ease while I put this book together, knowing that the virus will soon be gone, or put it this way, we have the medication to deal with this sickness. Stop.

We have to understand that there's enough creation for all Races to live on this Earth, but man wants to be greedy and have it all for himself, that's why there's so much division in the world. Resentment, hatred because the color of someone's skin. The world is always being destroyed. Understand that we bleed the same, if the lights were off through War you would not tell the difference who was bleeding, by holding onto hatred you are giving the enemy a ground to destroy the human race, to watch the shedding innocent lives through 9/11, how can a foreign country be jealous because of our cultures, our way of living? The enemy sits back and laughs, saying the stupidity of humans will destroy themselves. Republicans, Democrats, always at war with each other, denominational churches can never come on one Accord. Funny that the enemy can stay together, we can't while we're in this human flesh. Stop making the enemy's job so easy, let's act like we have some sense, I know the Coronavirus made everybody get some sense.

CHAPTER 11
Right or Wrong

THERE'S GOING TO BE A LOT OF PEOPLE THROUGHOUT THE WORLD going to learn things the hard way. No matter the color of your skin, you're going to be in for a rude awakening. I've learned that the Coronavirus is the New World Order, this is just the beginning of the Antichrist. Survival of the human race, dealing with your actions, against the New World Order. Do you know this is the doorway that is opening up for martial law, the number of the Beast, six-six-six. Is Trump in the White House for justice or injustice? There's a price to be paid. Are we dealing with greed or is it hatred to keep the American people in bondage, we will start to see more attacks on our soil, is the land cursed, is our government making wrong deals with foreign countries? Republicans and Democrats, take a look in the mirror, who's right or wrong in the way our country is going, does the United States and the foreign countries want to see the world collapse through pain and suffering? Dealing with problems Upon Our Land, news reporters like to keep the fire burning. The fire can be almost contained, but they want to start it back up, misery loves company, there's nothing wrong with you news reporters Keeping the Faith and praying for our country. Stop making a mockery out of everything, the world we live in is not a joke.

It's time for this country to have a better structure and Foundation, we need to learn how to line things up better, screen things more productively. We need a better system, tracking who comes to our land, too much traffic going in and out of the United States, especially the travel of foreign countries. Coronavirus is Airborne, made decades ago for the release of 2020. Scientists have been experimenting the virus for years, watching it grow.

From a baby to adult, released from a sore throat or cough, the cold or the flu. Do you know that the Coronavirus has always been airborne, ready to strike, waiting on his release? A virus that has been studied for decades, used to strike hot zones and cold zones. The hot zones New Jersey; New York; Los Angeles, California; Detroit, Michigan; New Orleans; Washington, D.C. Hot spots where people are aggressive, they have been targeted. The virus attacks the immune system and causes Havoc to the body. Coronavirus has been given a deadline to decrease WHILE it has increased. Scientists are testing the antidote to see how effective it will be. Experimentation has been going on for years to see what drug will neutralize the Coronavirus. Sea life of the animals, also the birds, lives of the animals. It was spread through the different birds that fly. Scientists have been able to control the virus to make it potent in different cities and states, the beginning of the New World Order viruses that are ready for the Armageddon War. Are the governments working on one Accord to form the New World Order? If another virus is released upon the world, is it going to study to see what city, states, and countries would crumble first? The 20 cities that are ready to go to work, they will take the number of the Beast easily, code zones. The Hot zones hit the hardest by the Coronavirus will resist.

When Donald Trump became president, people said that he had no experience in running the world. Yes, that might be true but the way Trump attacks is very aggressive, does he think before he reacts? Who knows what's going on in his mind, is he a firecracker that is ready to go off? Could we really have trusted Hillary Clinton as the first woman president? I guess the answer was no because she's not the president now, do you want to know the reasons why? Hillary Clinton was in a lot of business deals that affected the economy, she was stuck in the same system, her conduct was detrimental, business deals collapsing under the table. People kept blaming her for Obamacare, bad deals with stocks and bonds, supposedly extorting money. It was said that she has swindled millions of dollars, that was a red flag to the American people. So she could not be trusted in the White House, would she be able to deal with the heavy pressure by the decisions for the USA, how to run the Country Day in Day Out, and not show weakness in the midst of trials and tribulations no matter how hot the fire? Trump has a hard head to take a kicking and keep on ticking. Hillary Clinton talked a good game for the consumers to hear but didn't have enough loyalty for the American people. Hillary Clinton allowed other countries to grow off us, wasting tax-payers' money, if you follow her history it's all the same, cannot be trusted. Trump will help us find our identity, no more slipping and sliding. But gaining Traction in this world.

It's time for everybody to carry their weight, to get their hands dirty, just stand up and fight for this country. It's time to be the answer to the solution and not the problem, anybody with wrong motives, anything hiding in the dark that is causing problems, you will be brought to the light. Time to clean up homelessness, stop poverty, the different nationalities that are over here in the United States, come as you are, but Time For Peace. Nationalities that have businesses, it's time to interact with different races, it's time to balance the economy, by hiring different nationalities into your businesses. Stop racial division, we can all learn from each other, the different ethics of backgrounds. Embrace each other and not be prejudiced, we should all bring something new to the table that can benefit us. America is all about taking a chance to learn how to build together, so the economy can be successful. We have enough Nations over here in the United States to rebuild again, to make this land stronger and greater again, our corporations and businesses can learn to be productive if we teach each other. Money can continue to circulate throughout the United States if our economy is strong, Industrial factories, automobile factories, fruits and vegetable produce, cutting out the middleman and the third man, like foreign countries that think their formula of success is better than ours.

CHAPTER 12
Lullaby

WE MUST UNDERSTAND THERE IS GOING TO BE DARKNESS UPON THE LAND, evil is now surrounding the earth like never before. Mind, Body, heart, soul, it's going to be attacked. It's getting very hard to deal with the cares of the world. Struggling every day through trials and tribulations, you have to keep your mind guarded, understand stability, awareness of your strengths, relying on God Almighty. If you don't have a shelter for your mind, you will spend out of cycle. Problems arise, you must know how to go to the shelter to ease your mind so you will not have a spiritual breakdown. God Almighty with shelter, your mind, he will always give you Direction, in which way to go. Everybody's been put to the test dealing with the Coronavirus, if you haven't learned to keep your mind in perfect peace, you know what the art of suffering is. You must rise up through your emotions, and have a defense of survival mechanism of saying that you will survive. Especially if you have your children, hold down the fort and be strong, because they do not understand what's going on, and that's a shame about this whole ordeal of the Coronavirus, the children suffering, not able to play, to live life normally. We all should appreciate life more better after this is over with.

When the cares of the world get too heavy, we must go to God as a child, no matter how old you are, wondering when will the problem stop, Saying Daddy, Rock us in your arms, rock us so deep, rock us to sleep. Hush, Little Children, don't you cry, Daddy's going to sing you a lullaby. Dry those tears from your eyes, don't you worry about the sickness, don't you worry about the economy. Don't you worry about your mortgage, don't you worry about your businesses, don't you worry about your car notes. Hush, Little Children, don't you cry, take time to learn how to be still, how to meditate, how to be quiet. The whole world has been slowed down, a time to get your house in order, to forgive and forget, no longer holding grudges against family or friends. Through separation and distance we can examine ourselves, we all have something that can better ourselves. Problems won't last always. Joy comes in the morning. It's better to think positive than negative, faith is the substance of things not seen but things hoped for.

There is a fire upon earth that is burning up the infirmities. Everything that is bad is being burnt up. When fire strikes it becomes very dangerous, anything in its way will be destroyed. People don't like to stay in the fire, old saying if you can't stand the heat stay out the kitchen. There's a spiritual fire that is upon the Earth to bring about change. Very uncomfortable to the body when it strikes. As the fire burns it is putting things in order, the fire that Donald Trump is burning a blazing Heat. His fire will continue to burn until his job is done, right now no one is able to put out his fire, people have tried with the impeachment, now trying to slow down the presidential race for November. There's a spiritual fire that's attached to Donald Trump, it has been Godsent. How the fire has burned so strongly since he's been in the White House, a trailblazer, if he becomes president for another 4 years his work of Fire will be permanent on the minds of the American people. When President Trump displays his fireworks they are very colorful, a distinct signature like No other.

It is clear to see that Donald Trump has God's approval to be president of the United States. If you allow God to take you through the fire while dealing with Trump, you'll make it through. Chastisement is come upon the Earth for healing and deliverance, but if you get caught in the fire the first stage of smoke, you would not make it through. Understand the degrees of fire and the elements, when the fire turns a reddish orange you know that things are really cooking. Dissolving wrong motives, burning them up, dealing with prejudice, hate crimes, swindling American dollars to foreign countries. IRS overtaxing people, properties too high to rent to start businesses. People not receiving the same treatment as the next man, favoritisms towards another race, all Races and nationalities should be treated the same, these problems are going to challenge the president. Everybody Must Be purged for the truth, we all must fight the spirit of prejudice that comes in many forms and fashions. Let's stop pointing the finger at each other, let's work to become one, the heat can become unbearable or bearable, it all depends how you approach it.

Who is Donald Trump, what does he truly represent, no one can figure him out, there was a king in the Bible Days by the name of Nebuchadnezzar, the King was very ruthless, he wanted people to march to his tune. If you didn't follow the king's orders, you would be destroyed. Shadrach Meshach Abednego, thrown into the fiery furnace because they would not worship the king. The three men would not respond to what the king wanted them to do, he had the power to dictate at any given time. Is Donald Trump like Nebuchadnezzar, does he agree with the New World Order? Is he against anyone that stands for justice and Liberty, will he try to force the number of the Beast down our throats? Shadrach Meshach Abednego would not bow down to false gods. When they were in the fiery furnace, King Nebuchadnezzar said somebody else was in there that was the son of God. Three men came out of the fire, nothing was burnt on their bodies, you couldn't even Smell Smoke on them. King Nebuchadnezzar suffered many things because he did not follow God's instructions. Donald Trump will have to answer to God Almighty if he is not following his instructions, nobody is higher than God or greater than God or powerful than God. Remember, he is the creator of the universe, he raises one up and he puts one down, it's a dangerous thing to fall into the hands of Almighty God if you're being disobedient.

This season of Torment will be over soon concerning the Coronavirus, the economy is anxious to get back to work. People are starting to resist because they're ready to get back to work. Protesting is going on in Minneapolis, Minnesota; Detroit, Michigan; and Virginia, life civilizations ready to go on, people are tired of being shut up indoors. If the virus has been contained in areas and there's a decrease, why not get the American people back to working? Dictatorship of man wanting things his way, even if the tide is changing for the good, man still wants the worst. If there's no longer a threat in your city or state, take the shackles off our minds and our bodies. Just to let you know where I'm at in my thinking, it is April 19, 2020, still in the middle of the Coronavirus. Everything down now with the virus. This will always be in the back of our minds, nothing to hold on strong to but just a reminder the Coronavirus is the New World Order. Where do we truly go from here when this plague has passed? Can we appreciate this economy more better? I guess it was a nice thought for the stimulus checks to come to the American people, but that would never erase the many lives lost to the virus, rest in peace, everyone who has passed away.

CHAPTER 13
Responsibilities

WE ALL MUST BE AWARE OF OUR CIRCUMSTANCES IN LIFE, understand that we have a part to play in society in everyday living. The first second and third and fourth Generations, of our forefathers and mothers, put us in a hole. How we survive has become very damaging to the world. Poverty, homelessness, hunger, disease, famine in the land is the doing of the fore-fathers and mothers. Just like it is right now with the Coronavirus, dictator-ship and Leadership. Third-world countries destroyed by War, heavy rotation of violence, all manmade. To see the world suffer through man's hand, an act of hatred and Pride, no gratitude for life, how does it make people feel when they bring harm to our land, how can you go to sleep when you have destroyed lives? Are you completely cold blooded, there's no think-ing to your actions. Are you truly satisfied to be a menace to society, not thinking about the repercussions you have to deal with? Sooner or later your Consciousness will bring you down with your own Suicidal Thoughts, you created, there's no man or woman that can escape God, we all have to answer for our actions.

When it comes to the children, we are responsible for the way we live life. I'm tired of seeing children mistreated, will they have a future chance for hope? What does the Next Generation have to build on, nothing but a bunch of trash and Rubble, from war. We hear day in and day out about the third-world countries, no clean water, no food, no soft beds, the children have been left to defend because their parents have been killed in war, why should the little children suffer just like the Coronavirus, why does the chil-dren have to be involved, the children did not ask to come into this world, so why should they be afflicted, because of human ignorance, how can you bring something as precious into the world and watch it be defeated? Why destroy innocent lives, children have the right to be nurtured, to give them the right tools to succeed in life. America, please do not let this world turn into a third-world country, the collapse of the economy can make that happen. We all have the power to make this life a better place, live life positively, not negatively.

What is the right morals when it comes to raising children, it makes no sense for 13- and 14-year-olds to have babies. Clearly is evidence that children have not been raised with a functioning family. Girls were not taught to keep their legs shut to get the education and then get married. Stay away from mannish boys without the proper training to respect themselves and the girls, we cannot keep our eyes on the children 24/7 but if we take the time to educate them half the battle was won. Households do not have a solid foundation because the parents are never home, no guideline or structures to teach the children, they're left on their own. Teenagers turn to drugs and alcohol and hit the streets running hard, when pregnant 85 to 95% will not tell the parents but get an abortion, now life's reality is hit them in the face, no counseling, no one to walk it through with them. Stuck in a system of betrayal, finding out the boy doesn't want anything to do with her, now stuck in the emotions of having no life, barely knowing how to survive for yourself, dealing with peer pressure, embarrassed, depression, thinking that life cannot go on a worldwide epidemic for centuries, babies having babies, boys learning how not to become men but cowards, not facing life's responsibilities. 40 years old, out on the streets.

Don't blame the children when they become adults, saying they're no good. Every time you turn around they're always in and out of jail, not able to live a productive life. Take a look at the mirror, you are an example of how they were raised when they were kids. A lot of responsibilities have been put on the kids at an early age basically to raise themselves, because the parents are out doing their thing, the kids are not being monitored, so the same monkey that's on the parents' back is on children's back. Sex, drugs, and rock and roll, or rhythm and blues or hip-hop. Parents are too busy chasing the thrill while the children are left open to society. They become affected, Stuck in a Pandora's Box, the wrong way to live life. In raising children there must be rules and regulations so the children will learn discipline, to understand Authority. The problem with a lot of children and teenagers and adults in and out of the system at early ages, no respect for the law. Children only follow their parents or what they see somebody else do, remember the children are always listening and looking. It's in their DNA to follow what we say and do. It's our responsibility to raise them up right.

If you take a look out the window all you see is poverty, drugs, prostitution and gangs. We all have to be held accountable for the things that we have done good or bad. Destructive Behavior, man tearing this Earth up, God did not design the world to be corrupt, the streets filthy, corruption everywhere, man has brought sickness to the body. God gave man dominion over everything, to live off the Earth, to cultivate the land, but the sin through man has brought a curse to the Earth. Everything has become contaminated, by disobedience, man's true nature to tear up the Earth. No, we will always deal with the threat of tsunamis, tornadoes, volcanoes and earthquakes. So when we face calamities don't point the finger at God. Just like the Coronavirus, manmade, now we need a merciful god, to take this plague away from us. Thank God Almighty that he's giving the scientists the right antidote to defeat the virus, God could have thrown in the towel on man because he was the one that put out this virus, but God's mercy and Grace upon his children is a blessing, I know that many lives have been lost. Don't worry, whoever is behind this, you reap what you sow.

The United States can still be a beautiful country if we learn how to live together, don't let man destroy this Earth, there's more love than evil. Love is the key to satisfaction at the end of the day, love will prevail. Right now the world is displaying love, helping each other outdo these unpredictable times. 2020 has taken Everybody by storm. What a powerful impact the world is facing. We must show who we really are, crybabies or strong Warriors. Our fight is physically dealing with the immune system, we also have the fight against the mind. God has not given us a spirit of fear but of love and of a sound mind, keep your mind renewed in these days, understanding that we will make it through this season of drought and despair. Trouble doesn't last always, even though we do not know the time frame. Stay in the Gap from one another at a distance, love and pray for one another, truly knowing in your mind this will pass. I will be giving you important information, a blueprint on how we must build in the United States. Freedom of speech, Equal justice, Liberty for all, a right to live life civilized. Our lives have been shaken to the Core, whatever things have slowed you down in life, or what you need to stop, or get better in. Now's the Time to turn the corner.

CHAPTER 14
Racial Prejudice

WE TRULY UNDERSTAND THAT HISTORY WAS MADE, Barack Obama was President. Did it change the course of the world, to a certain degree, did it stop the oppression and depression? Barack Obama became the first black president in the White House, that did not sit well with a lot of Americans, it definitely rubbed a lot of people the wrong way, a lot of people were in shock displaying hatred, no gratitude, but it gave the minorities a sense of relief, your time to shine, Proud To Be An American. The people could walk with their heads High, understanding that they are equal, it really changed the course of life, first of all you have to understand that it took a majority of white Americans to vote for Barack Obama, a changing of the guards that a minority could be president. Understanding no longer a slave mentality but the right to have a piece of the land, dignity, understanding that no one is better than any other, no more splitting up, everybody playing with the same baseball in the same park. Days of segregation should be torn out of the history books. It truly was amazing to see Barack Obama in the White House for 8 years.

Barack Obama was President, Prejudice was shut down, people were given a clean slate to walk freely, to be a productive citizen to own land and properties. Doorways being open, minorities can no longer say where's my 40 acres and a mule. Freedom of opportunity has been given to you, now work the land, stop having your hands out looking for free handouts. Everybody had an opportunity to grow while Obama was in the White House, but if you have been sitting back pointing fingers for 8 years, and not accomplishing anything that's your fault. God made the playing field equal. All Nations and races to enjoy. If you did not take advantage of this great blessing, to establish yourself on this Earth, wake up. Martin Luther King had a dream and a vision, one day we would all be equal as one, and we have seen this come to pass by Barack Obama being president of the United States. Something I can tell my children as they tell their children passed down from generation to generation.

Now that President Trump is on the scene, is racial prejudice back in the making? Minorities have been shot down, especially black Americans, by police officers, a random act of violence. 90% of the victims had no weapons on them, shot down like deer in a Hunting Expedition. Black lives do matter, all lives matter, the imprint has been put back on the world. Take a stand against prejudice or a corrupt government system, people that are above the law. It's time for all nations and races to step up to the plate if you're living in the United States. You came to this country, you got what you wanted, don't sit in your businesses and talk about the calamities that this world is facing. Donald Trump is challenging all nationalities and races over here in the USA. You have migrated over here to the USA because of dictatorship, now you're running scared in this country. Everything that you do is now being exploited, welcome to the party, the way Donald Trump looks at you minorities, foreigners, everything about your properties and homes will be put to the test, there's no longer time to be arrogant choosing sides against another race, now you're riding in the same boat, is it a taste of your own medicine?

Now that you foreigners are coming to the United States to set up shop to live in our country, you are now responsible to help this country grow. You've been over here for decades, trying to adapt to our ways of living, sitting back and shaking your heads, talking about what the country goes through, now it's time to use your freedom of speech. The dictatorship that you ran from in your country is trying to come across to our great land. You have the right to plead the Fifth Amendment, you have the right to smile, the right to express yourself. You have been given a platform of success, you have really made something of yourself, now give back to the land, you have had a chance to taste of this good land and you know the United States is the greatest country to live in. You can wake up in the morning or go to sleep at night, not worried about a government system that can destroy everything you worked so hard to build. You can relax with your loved ones, not worried about the dictatorship of War. It would be a crying shame, everything that you work so hard for in the United States, it's gone at the drop of a dime. You have taken over the name Americans when you came to this great country, no matter what nationality you might be.

It's time to stop hiding your hatred towards Americans, discrimination, wrong motives of thinking. Don't be quick to jump on somebody else's bandwagon to ride with them before looking at the real situation, don't go off looks first, you must examine something to see if it's real or not. Don't be caught up with the wrong benefactor leading you down the wrong path. There's no longer time to sit back to be hypocritical of the next man or woman, especially if he's staying side by side you for safety, knowing that you both believe in the same standards, learn how to understand that the proof is in the pudding, it doesn't take a genius to see Donald Trump is on a whole different level. If he cannot get you to jump when he says jump, then you are very dangerous to him. Just like a lion, he's looking for the weakest one in the pack, someone that will bow down to him that won't go against what he says, no matter if he's right or wrong. Foreigners over here, are you the weakest link or do you have power to stand with your fellow man? Fight for equality, most of all for our loved ones and our children.

We don't know how long civilization will last on Earth, we must always be prepared for disaster to come across the United States. 9/11 was something that the world is never truly recovered from, it was a dose of reality, shocking fear, something that brought all the nations together, but the ones that it didn't affect like the people in foreign countries living in the United States, with the attitude saying oh well, we've dealt with that for many years in our country. It's a part of life, you really need to check yourself, it should not be mass destruction anywhere. With that type of attitude, you should not be in the United States, why would you wish harm to anybody? Foreigners that have escaped that lifestyle of living to come to the USA, if you have the mentality that we deserve it that's a part of War, you're mistaken. Is it because we have let you come to the United States and you have brought disaster upon our land? Have you been plotting and planning for decades to destroy our soil, not pointing fingers at any nationality or race over here but just letting it be known? If you think we should suffer because you have suffered in your foreign countries, you're wrong. Don't come over here taking advantage of our systems to think that we are weak and immature. Americans know how to come together and fight when our backs are against the walls, dealing with the Coronavirus. Americans are showing we have power, there is great strength in numbers, pulling together the American way.

CHAPTER 15
Foreigners

FOREIGNERS KNOW HOW TO RESIST, they come from a culture that will fight for their freedom of democracy, they have escaped a lifestyle of shootings and bombings, suicide forced by dictatorship. Foreigners have come to the United States with the scars on their minds and their backs how their country has treated them. People being held in bondage to corrupt government, no say-so on how to live life but being bullied forced to live in the system. Pretty much martial law government that controls their welfare, Life, giving strict guidelines to who you can worship or not. Families living in Beatdown shelters, barely enough food to survive, diseases and famine throughout the land, government living comfortably, clean water to drink, excellent food to eat, fathers being beaten and thrown in jail, little girls and mothers being raped, sold through sex trafficking, children no green grass to play on, muddy dirt roads, garbage and trash everywhere.

Foreigners living over here in the United States refuse to engage in structural matters concerning the United States, they would not stand up and fight for our rights, injustice going on in the land. They learn how to turn their heads, looking the other way as they laugh, but now that Donald Trump is president he's pushing up on all nationalities in the United States. So everybody is now being challenged, treated unfairly with the president displaying Prejudice towards a different race. Time to stand up for the land, you have been given $30,000 or more to start your businesses, while you debate in your coffee shops talking about the Americans, you understand dictatorship and Leadership, it doesn't feel good for a government system to rule you, but you cannot have freedom of speech or have the right to agree or disagree, but now you're over here in the United States with an attitude saying you would not fight for the American people, while your revenues, companies and businesses are doubling your quota, earn income every year. You learn how to work the system and also to get over where the taxpayer is paying double of his hard-earned wages.

I'm not saying that all foreigners living in the United States are being negative, but you know who you are that is polluting the system, to have the right to freedom of living is now being threatened, making room for the New World Order. There is a method to Madness, it is fighting for a right to be free in the land. Without any type of bondage. Single mothers are barely surviving, getting enough from the system, living off of general assistance. Rich stay Rich, poor stay poor. The foreigners get more loans than the American people that live over here. A lot of the neighborhoods are poverty-stricken. Abandoned buildings, the government refuses to tear them down, but there is a liquor store on every block with foreigners running it, pretending that they are our brother or sister, they have no problem, poison the community, whatever it takes for them to build, if that means going to the ghetto, having a mentality that they are better than us, and we are beneath them. Foreigners over here from different nationalities with businesses cannot hide their demeanor, especially when they have shops in the so-called ghetto, they will take your money, they will display a look of prejudice upon their face.

Foreigners need to understand there's a New World Order approaching us and we must all come together as one. When the Smoke Clears at the end of the day you are still a minority. No matter how you clean yourself up, you are just a number, just like the other minorities in the United States, black Americans, the treatment that they've been receiving for decades, your turn is right around the corner, now that Donald Trump is president he wants to dictate, especially foreigners in the United States. Trump will bring the hammer down on all foreigners, you will be exploited. Join the bandwagon with the other minorities because a lot of you foreigners have been treated like dirt, you will have to fight hard to keep your businesses, to make sure you are legally supposed to be here. So if all nationalities and foreigners come together, we will have the opportunity to succeed in life. We will not be bullied through martial law, told when to wake up or to go to sleep. A lot of foreigners are playing kickball the way the government wants you to kick the ball, if you're no standards they will shut you down, so they want you to stay in the hood with your keeping minorities in bondage.

In order to receive your businesses a lot of foreigners have been brainwashed, to make sure you are superior to the other minorities. You come to this great land not appreciating the pathway that the other foreigners have set starting with black Americans. I'm not pointing the finger at you, but I'm letting you know in order to be successful don't look at the color of the skin. Look at the better side of people, no matter what you heard or Been Told, everybody deserves a chance. Every nationality and race has been talked about, underneath the Sun. Regardless if it's true or not, don't judge the next person, take time to see for yourself, if you find out he is what he is then leave him alone. When you see somebody you cannot always think that he's always up to no good in and out of trouble. If that's the case, if our government went off looks, a lot of you foreigners would not be over here now, our government should have screened foreigners better coming over here. Not to say that they put a spell on our land, that we should suffer with a dictator leader like their countries have no peace of mind. How can you come to the great country still being prejudiced and jealous of our system? It's people like you that don't deserve to be over here, you cannot have your cake and eat it too.

Being a foreigner in the United States, you are considered the underdog, not the elites, no matter how hard you work, no matter what credentials you have you are still considered average. Keep in mind any time that you do not play according to the rules, you can be shut down for good, no matter what time you put into your craft, no matter how many people you have on your team, you can become distinct. So don't get your hopes up even though you get your back rubbed at times, saying you have become an outstanding citizen. When the New World Order strikes the power that you thought you have was just fake, pretend. Understand that you will be in the same boat, in the same predicament like everybody else, plenty of people have worked hard and sacrificed for this great country, but if you don't take the number of the Beast your hard work means nothing, it is said that even loved ones will turn on you, and turn you in. It would be in your best interest to take a stand with your fellow man to strive for equality. Since dealing with the Coronavirus, Armageddon War seems to be closer than what we thought it was. All nationalities are welcome in the USA, To Join the Revolution. Going through the Coronavirus, we see how the shackles are on our feet that man has created. Everything was designed to study the human race to see how we respond to disaster, to see how the economy would be affected, to see how people respond to following orders. I know that a lot of foreigners have escaped your country to come to the USA to get away from bigotry. As American people we will not be forced into concentration camps or slaughtered like pigs, it is time for somebody to crack the code, now it's on, this is what the Coronavirus has brought, out to the table.

CHAPTER 16
Resistance

It's time for the resistance Army, be strong from City to City, block to block in the United States. We will not tolerate bullying for Isis or Al-Qaeda or the government. We will protect our families as a unit, we will March in order to our own tune. We will know who enters our streets from block to block, it is time to know your neighbors, if we all pull together as one we will be able to survive better as a nation. More outbreaks will come upon the land, this time we'll be prepared and more ready, where every Community will have a grip on civilization. We must have designated areas, food, water, toilet paper, medicine, everything needed to survive, every block should Network in order to make it through any storm we go through, it's time for the neighborhoods to be strong. If we have a system of living down it would make things easier for us to survive, our job is to protect our neighborhoods. Every block can be guarded and watched out for, if we designate Homes and Apartments on the Blocks, to be Refuge centers, to make sure everybody on the Block is taken care of in the middle of any crisis that we face. We shouldn't have to leave anywhere to get medicine, Food, Water, Supplies, everything will be right there in the community. Doctors, nurses, dentists, farmers, mechanics, this is very important that we have these people in our community, it depends on our survival.

United States is a Multicultural Nation, it's going to take all nations to stand as one time, to stand up for our rights, to understand the Warfare of the Mind, if you have not understood the whole Coronavirus epidemic your eyes are being blinded, it's the beginning of the New World Order, or testing protocol to see who will Bow Down. Be prepared for battle, spiritually, mentally, physically. I'm not saying that we are vigilantes but the resistance that will fight for our rights. People have been protesting for years when they've had injustices in their land, treated unfairly, discrimination, together we will be unstoppable, this is what's going to make the community strong. It is designed to cast out any bias for any kind of racism or War or dictatorship of a New World Order, how can we bring about change in our homes and in our streets, understanding the foundation of our history? All nationalities and races over here in the United States, the reason that you're over here is now to work together to resist dictatorship through bondage.

How has the world become so dysfunctional because the family traits have been thrown out the door, no balance in the families when one parent is in the household is a disadvantage to the children, not having a father to run the household, kids become dysfunctional, heading towards the streets or violence. The boys become involved in gangs, the girls become at a great risk to get pregnant, a disadvantage by not having both parents in the household. In today's society the kids have grown up with the emotional scars and baggage. You develop a dictating spirit, The Taste for hatred. Because you have been given a strong power of position. Whatever office is might seem to be Supreme Court, Republicans, Democrats, mayor, president, what morals were you raised in when you were a child? Not being happy, looking at injustice, nothing but violence all around you, hatred and jealousy and pride and arrogance, becoming like Hitler, dictating a whole population, especially in foreign countries, where everybody has to bow down to you walking on eggshells, no one to fight for their rights except terrorists that don't understand Equal justice, all they think about is destroying man, woman, and children.

We will resist and take a stand against Injustice, the American people are not dogs trained to follow the government's commands. When people get tired of doing something they don't want to do they resist. People were starting to protest and move around, because they're tired of being shut in because of the Coronavirus. It's like they'd rather take their chances against the virus, knowing that's not the right thing, but at the same time taking a stand to go back to civilization, understand the chips will fall where they fall, even though that is a bold statement, but we must get back to Everyday Life. The American people have heart and soul, our prayers and condolences go out to the ones that lost their life, we have to find a solution, if the virus is decreasing in different states then go back to work, stop having a dictating spirit. Resistance is formed for a reason to combat martial law to understand our freedom of Liberty, to understand the severity of a matter, to weigh the options to see if we are not being bullied or dictated. We will not bow down or put into quarantine for no reason, freedom of Liberty, freedom of speech to make sure our voices are being heard. War is truly something that the world cannot Escape but we do not have to engage in war, but we do have the right to protect our loved ones and our families. Protection is very important in these trying days, we need wisdom and knowledge, it's going to take all nationalities and races to pull together to have each other's backs.

Raising a family is very important, we must understand our children, we must give the teenagers a platform to speak, it's by our mistakes they've been damaged, the children that were born in the millennium or the Next Generation, they truly have a voice. Take time to listen to your children, get in their business, it's important to have family time at least three times out of the week. Children need to know that they are loved, believe me, it makes a big difference in life. Generations growing up today are watching every move, we make a picture of our society. All the nationalities of different races over here in the United States, stop trying to twist our laws and be Prejudice of our lifestyles. There's nothing wrong with bringing your Traditions here but don't resist against ours. Stop being rude and obnoxious, talking very loud in your language as if you're better than us, as if you have a secret to say, acting like we are toxic. There's nothing wrong with speaking in your language, but when you do it deliberately acting like you're prejudice. We don't need you over here, at least try to talk some English in front of Americans. Stop being so bold like that you know exactly what I'm saying, we have enough hatred in the world today, we need each other to combat any attack that comes across our soil, we need to have more neighborhood watch programs, take it an extra step further to make sure everybody on our block is taken care of. Food, water, bathroom supplies, everything we need to survive medicine.

The different nationalities living in the United States, stop being conformed to oppression and depression from your country. Things that you did over there will not work over here, especially your lifestyle. You have no right to get mad because your sons and daughters want to leave their tradition of dressing to dress like Americans. Let your children Express themselves, don't keep them in bondage, they have a right to dress as American citizens, what's the reason for coming to the United States if your children can be free, they have a right to dress as Americans, stop keeping your wives held hostage with old traditions that don't matter that you had back in your country. Allow your wives and women and children to get out of the houses, allow them to make friends. This is why you're in the United States, for freedom, stop abusing your women, they are not a bunch of dogs but humans just like you are, there's too many dysfunctional families from foreign countries, stop treating your women and children like slaves, they've been dictated long enough. So what if they want to listen to rhythm and blues, rock and roll, jazz, Hip-Hop, they have a right to, stop making your women and children live beneath you, it is pathetic, if there was a law saying that all foreign women can leave their husbands because of bondage to traditional ways. I guarantee you 80% to 90% of the women will be gone. It's time to understand your fellow man, war is on the horizon, we must be ready as one nation, the resistance.

CHAPTER 17
Community Clean-up

It's time for the resistance to build the United States, the movement of the resistance is designed to set up structure for the American people. Time to invest in each other, all nationalities in the United States. It's all about equal justice, time to sit down at the table to discuss what we can do to make our families better, to bring change to the environment, but having your own business you could teach self-improvement to the American people. Learn how to cultivate the land when dealing with problems. Point out your Mishaps, struggles, turn around and disappointment in life, unlock the doors of your heart and soul, you can become successful in anything you put your mind to do, build a circle of men and women to invest in each other, to generate money, to take care of each other. Equal Unity is very important to build in communities to develop a bond of trust.

If we learn how to understand each other's weaknesses, strengths, we can learn how to build as a nation. We can learn how to improve as a people individually and together to make the resistance strong, pulling together, we will not have to depend on the government system that will try to defeat us. It's going to take diligence and perseverance to make every Community strong. Communication is the key to reward each other, to know our neighbors from block to block, we must step out of Oppression and depression, breaking the cycle of dictatorship, leadership from the government. If we learn how to stop the self-destruction on our blocks, and build a resistance to protect each other, everybody wins. We have to understand that the children need a safe environment, the Next Generation needs a platform for right standards of everyday living. We need to have places of Refuge in the community, Tranquility to know that there's hope, just like dealing with the Coronavirus, people are pulling together to help their fellow man, no longer looking at the color of skin or the nationality, pulling together, strong Americans understanding that a pandemic is a very serious thing, it doesn't care about a color.

Now is the right time for the resistance to get our houses in order. Time for the resistance to get our house in order, to stand against a New World Order, we're dealing with a manmade virus designed to dictate the world, to rule the world, the system wants the world to stay in panic and in fear. The Beast wants to create martial law across the land with strict restrictions, resistance is designed to take care of family and friends if there is Injustice in the world. If the government wants to put us in bondage, knowing that they are wrong, but still want to abuse their power, we'll take a stand for freedom of speech, freedom of our rights and freedom of Liberty, the resistance, there has been just a little bit of percussion in dealing with the Coronavirus, on how Americans should distance themselves from each other. Whatever it takes for us to beat this virus but whatever guidelines and restrictions that you know are not fair, in the future you will not get away with that. Community clean-up, we have a greater fight that is now starting to surface in the United States, the New World Order dictatorship to rule the nation, the number of the Beast 666, the stealing, robbing, fighting, the drugs, prostitution, everything in neighborhoods that is wrong, let's clean it up. Time to get rid of negativity in our communities. Warfare is on the rising, dictatorship telling the American people when they can eat, sleep, and you will know what else.

The resistance is here to be a solution to everyday life problems. Stop contaminating the streets, understand their mind, body, heart, and soul, what were the circumstances that brought destruction, a life of poverty, homelessness, wrong direction in life, no father figure, lending a helping hand to clean up our communities, we can defeat the cycle of wrong circumstances, if we have a code of honor to respect each other, to be there for each other when dealing with trials and tribulations. We can take back our cities from block to block, maybe we can't change the whole world, but the ones that agree you can't go wrong! Truly know that this movement is from God Almighty, he will clean out the blocks that are designed to have Refuge. If people understand the enemy that we all face, doesn't care about the color of our skin. Get that through to our heads, then we will understand all nationalities and races, we are the resistance in the USA. There should be safety zones throughout the communities on every block, by networking letting people know if they move from City to City or from state to state they know exactly what their neighborhoods are made of, a great tool to recruit families looking for a safe place of Refuge, protection for the children, knowing exactly what the block has to offer. To develop a Bond like this is going to be very important for the survival of the human race.

It's time to create an open field growth in the neighborhoods. People need to feel good about the communities that they have the right lifestyle of living on their blocks. Resistance is an extension of the neighborhood watch, our foundation is built on God Almighty, taking a stand in the spiritual first by praying and watching results second in the physical, binding and rebuking and casting out, strongholds that might be in your neighborhood. No matter what type of traffic that is in your neighborhood, if everybody learns how to pray we will defeat the enemy, and run them right off the block, by the resistance being on one Accord we are powerful enough to watch the movement of God Almighty clean up the atmosphere. Remember God wants to keep us safe to build a refuge for all nationalities, coming together with garage sales, cupcake sales, BBQs, trash cleanups, Community meetings two or three times out the month. By doing this you are changing the atmosphere, where the light will outshine the darkness. That is showing love, which would defeat any enemy by people pulling together, showing love and affection, we can defeat any virus or catastrophe. If we use the same formula in anything in life living, we become winners. When the whole world prays together we can defeat anything, no matter what this world is facing, to the believer and unbeliever, if you take a chance you will see the results. I know the world is tired of suffering due to the Coronavirus, so it will not hurt if you take a chance to pray. When people's backs are against the wall they'll try anything, why not try God? I give you the keys to unlock the Mysteries of everyday life and how to defeat the enemy. When you pray spiritual warfare will be done in the spiritual Realm, anything in your neighborhoods, gangs, drugs, prostitution, stealing will cease. The battle will now be in God's hands, not our hands, he will defeat any enemy that comes against us. When the whole world understands this, we would not have to suffer for so long dealing with calamities.

If we change our thought patterns about our neighbors, we can begin to change wrong patterns in our community. Instead of looking out your window at your neighbors, trying to figure them out while you talk about them, be positive and pray for them, believe that their intentions are good, that they are productive citizens. I know that there's a lot of stay-at-home mothers. Set a pattern to be peaceful, tea parties or women's night out, it's always good to network with your neighbor or to email or to talk on the phone. Special codes will be made for houses and apartments to let us know that you are part of the resistance. We will have designated areas where children can play without being in danger as somebody watches over them. Every house and apartment will have a walkie-talkie when dealing with Code Reds. Trouble On The Block, people in need of food, shelter, transportation, conducting meetings, to have a signal of a radius to keep track of the children as they play, emergencies if somebody gets hurt. All nationalities understand what it means to be homeless, hungry, sick. We all struggle with the same symptoms in this fleshly body day in and day out, take time to work on our problems, we may disagree or agree but to come into an agreement without fighting, the destruction of humankind wanting to dictate has always brought on War, just like the Great War, the Armageddon, USA, Russia, Syria, Israel, China, watch out for the manifestation. All the people that like to hang out on the Block, we can incorporate them if they believe in our vision, they can be security for the block. We could hire them to protect our children, grandparents to make sure they have a safe passage to leaving the house and going back into the house, they will become our eyes and ears because they're on the Block, so they know exactly what's coming to the block. The favor of God will be upon us for change in the communities, the hustlers on the Block, panhandlers, gangs will see that the resistance is for security. When the gangs and the cartels understand the fight is not with each other but against a New World Order that wants to dictate man, they will join our side and stand up for the communities. I'm getting this message to the whole world, we need each other, all nationalities in the USA. I don't care who you are or what you're into, all nations and races, please read this book to understand what we're facing as a nation.

CHAPTER 18
World Turns

THERE'S A CHANGING OF THE GUARD, the whole world is going through a crisis, everything changed when Trump became president. It's time for the denominations to wake up all religions on the face of the Earth. Democrats, Republicans, take a look in the mirror, nothing is new underneath the sun when it comes to people fighting for their rights. Jim Jones, David Koresh, we're all about the protection from mankind, but they wanted to be gods becoming demonically possessed, their blueprint and methods of thought seem to be right but God did not tell them to move his children. Once again wanting to dictate, to be better than the next person, greed and vengeance. It's going to take Revival to sweep the land for the resistance to stop calamities, sickness and disease, martial law. It's going to get to the point that humans are going to be put in Chains, dictating how to live our lives, no Liberty, no freedom of speech, no right to explore the land, strict restrictions, living life. The whole world is wondering exactly what Donald Trump possesses, is he a trouble starter, will there be problems every time he turns around, especially if he becomes president for another 4 years? The 4 years that he has been in the White House has been very different, the whole world is uncertain of his methods.

Nobody knows when the Armageddon war is going to happen, but one thing I do know Donald Trump is kicking the ball, things are starting to happen, the world is unpredictable. Barack Obama did his eight years in the White House, a lot of people said that he didn't get anything accomplished. He took down Bin Laden, that was good for the American people, but now that he is no longer president racism is now at the top of the charts. Obama was faced with many issues being the president of the White House, dealing with the Supreme Court, not getting the right money that he needed to make this world better. A lot of people say that he made the economy better, a lot of people said he made the economy worse. I know that it had to be like pulling teeth when Obama had to deal with the Supreme Court. Donald Trump is always challenging the Supreme Court, giving them a run for their money, before the New World Order strikes hard the resistance will be in place, right now it's about looking out for the Next Generation, the children need a foundation to build off. We cannot leave them to defend for themselves in the dark.

Everything is different right now in the world today, all nationalities that are over here in this land, there's going to be a great deficit that you will suffer, economically and physically, the transferring of your wealth, it's going to be very difficult to reach your people to try and bring them over here, nobody knows how long the economy will suffer, or when it will pick up again. Be thankful that you're over here, so now take a look how you can better yourself or the country. How can we bring about change with a diversified country? We are very different cultures and backgrounds, this economy can become strong. There's no need for other countries to come over here to occupy Our Land, we will have the strongest light shining in the world because we are unique. We have the best resources ever, Two Become One. Donald Trump is taking a stand, other countries know that we are not weak and pathetic. We are starting to come into power now that Trump is behind the wheel. We have to learn to understand the beauty of the land, if you cultivate the land through love this world would be very successful. If you stay in anger and pride through arrogance the world would be destroyed. Wisdom and knowledge is a very important thing, you have to know the state of your flock in order to see which way the world is going.

If you don't understand the rules to our land you shouldn't be here, you're not welcome. Blood and Tears have been spilled over this great nation, everybody is responsible for their actions. I'm talking about the different nationalities over here, our life has been very different than yours. A lot of you come from a Bad life of corruption, dealing with evil and vicious men, not having your freedom of dignity or speech, we watch the news and read the newspapers, how foreign countries treat their people like trash, also keeping people hostage, abandoned homes of children suffering, no food, no clean water, pestilence everywhere. We must continue to work hard in the United States to not become like a third-world country. Once again, why should the little children suffer, where is the remorse, why destroy an innocent life? Third-world countries are destroyed because of man's egotistical ways, we cannot allow the debacle of the United States, if our economy fails us it will be a quick New World Order. The government system wants to see the world in shambles, that way they can dictate concentration camps. Pockets of poverty and homelessness popping up throughout the United States. When the government sees abandoned buildings it's a win on their side, they will not fix up the buildings, they want this world to collapse, to take the number.

If mass destruction comes upon the land there's not going to be any electricity, no place to rest, no shelter, no food, this will be the beginning of the number of the Beast and martial law, dictatorship, heavy upon the land, a world of Doom and Gloom. People talk about the Rapture taking place before the New World Order, planes will fall out the sky, trains and cars will crash, everybody that is saved will be gone. Darkness will be in the land, whoever is not saved will be down here on this Earth, it's going to be a lot of people stuck down here on this Earth, that finally realized the Rapture was true. How will you defend for yourself, how will you be able to fight against the Beast? I will not elaborate about this too much, there's plenty of books about the New World Order. It's up to you to believe it or not, that's what's so good about this nation, you have the right to agree or disagree. Me myself, I know that this is true. There's going to be a lot of martyrs left down on this Earth. To the gangs and cartels, you have been warned about this chain of events. Even though I do not know what lifetime this will be in, but I know that is very close. 5 years, 10 years, 15 years, it could be sooner because the Coronavirus does spell the New World Order. Destruction that man has brought upon the Earth, and I know that this is just the beginning, so we have to be prepared and ready as a people, the resistance we will take a stand for one another As the World Turns.

Everybody wants to know, is this the beginning of trials and tribulations? I don't know but it sure feels like it. The whole world has got a taste of 2020, it sure doesn't feel good. I was not able to celebrate my daughter's birthday, stuck in the house, the only thing to do is to write this book. Looking at the world is very different now, survival will always be in the front of my mind first, which it always has been, but life has gotten way more serious now. I've trained my mind to think of the Coronavirus as an everyday thing, but I know it will pass with the grace of God. Until then I'm learning how to adapt to the world we're living in now. I'm content but not satisfied. I'm living life like I have no more chances, so I'm making the best out of it, enjoying my loved ones and Friends, finding things to laugh about, telling people that I'm sorry that I owe apologies to. I'm learning how to pray and how to put up with people more, not letting people get on my nerves easily but to embrace change to be there for people in need. Somebody has to be strong because if we all give up the world would never have a chance to survive any epidemic. Faith is the key to endurance, standing in the gap for people, being aware of any circumstance. Knowing that there is a solution to any problem, understanding You're never alone.

CHAPTER 19
Refuge

We must set up positions of Refuge throughout the United States for protection in these troubling days. We must be ready for war, the first war came to an end in 1918, Over 21,528,000 civilians died. Over 21,189,000 were hurt after the atom bomb. Hiroshima, Nagasaki brought World War II to an end, men, women, and children, 60,000,000 dead in the streets. War will repeat itself again, what generation was suffering through communism, is the United States in a deficit, do we owe foreign countries billions of dollars? Is this the reason that dictatorship will be enforced to gain power and wealth by any means necessary? It is designed to shake the core of this great land, the government revenues of money, the spending of American dollars is out of control. Stimulus checks will put a big dent in the economy, it's designed for the collapse of the American people, down the road, everything is designed for the economy to continue to take hits. If the American people run out of money, is it all designed to be broke, to depend on foreign country diplomatic immunity? How much money is the United States spending right now for research against the Coronavirus, extra money to get the antidote from foreign countries?

It is a spirit of nimrod in the White House, has the Supreme Court created a tyranny in the White House? To build the New World Order with the spirit of nimrod, trying to be higher than God. If you have not heard the story of nimrod you need to do your research. Nimrod was trying to get everybody on one Accord to build a tower, to reach God in the heavens. Genesis 11:14, a combination of all Races and Nations coming together to be unstoppable, to establish a one-world order dictatorship. Is the White House trying to stick with the same beliefs of the forefathers from the third, fourth, and fifth generation, can we depend on the government economically, socially, or religiously? Man is not higher than God, just like Nimrod, God had to destroy the tower to switch around the languages so the people were not on one Accord. Pagan worship is getting stronger in the White House, is the Supreme Court and occult. When Donald Trump became president he did not only have to deal with the American people but the Supreme Court for what they stand in and Believe on. Donald Trump's beliefs are different, it is said that they pray to the bones of their forefathers in the White House, The Supreme Court.

Nimrod was a pagan worshipper, Nimrod was seen as God the father of the Sun. Legends say that Nimrod died in his prime, leaving Queen Semiramis by herself, it has been said that Nimrod became immortal. His Spirit flew to the Sun, taking charge, beelsamen, Lord of Heaven, the sun god. Nimrod impregnated his Queen through a Sunbeam being a virgin, had a son that was born December 25th, Tammuz. His mother became the East star or Venus immortal. Tammuz was known as the vegetable God. When he died all the vegetation died also, by being resurrected in the spring he was considered the lord of the Dead. He was supposed to be The Rebirth of the humankind. Pagan worship has been in the White House for centuries, it is now out of control in the White House, the government wants to take the Place of the Father, Son, and the Holy Spirit, the enemy wants to infiltrate himself as the Creator to take the place of the trinity. Ezekiel Chapter 8, verse 14 through 16, talks about this abomination. It is now starting to take over the White House, the New World Order, the number of the Beast, six-six-six.

The government wants to force Pagan worship on the face of the Earth and not to believe in God we trust. Dictatorship from the government is trying to force the rules of the forefathers. Antichrist is setting up shop, everybody and everything is being targeted, waiting for the collapse of all Nations to bring about a one-world order. The government wants to keep the same system running in place, the same foundations laid day in and day out. For Bush Senior and his son to become president, who would have thought that would ever happen? Antichrist wants to keep his momentum going strong. Will history repeat itself again with any of the former presidents having a family-run to be president in the future? Donald Trump understands the principalities in the White House, will he follow God's lead or the Antichrist's lead? I know that Trump is butting heads, he must keep the faith to make a tremendous sacrifice for the American people. Presidents in the White House before he was in there followed the rules of the Supreme Court, bowing down to the Beast.

We already know that man cannot be trusted, if God did not have his hand upon the USA man would have destroyed the world a long time ago. You must watch out for a corrupt system that wants to keep us oppressed and depressed to the foreigners living over here, you've raised your children from generation to generation in this great land. You own property and businesses, you can freely go and come as you choose. Do you love your freedom being over here in this country, so let's take a stand together so we will not be dictated, we need to have the cooperation of the foreigners, everybody has the right to express themselves, not to be loaded down with the weights of Destruction. You must be ready to fight against a system that wants to destroy equal rights. We are all in this together to make sure we all have a safe Refuge. If we are being challenged, it sure feels good to go down together, swinging all nationalities together, the American people have no problems with you foreigners being over here, you have children that had children from the third, fourth, and fifth generation. You have made a strong Mark in this land, you have established a reputation as being American.

There's going to be a bill passed called Office of Religious Persecution Monitoring. When the bill goes into effect everybody will be dictated, especially denominational churches, you will be tried and put through the fire. If you are not following the standards or guidelines of the Constitution, you will be shut down. People that have Investments with stocks and bonds, renting buildings for businesses, or only land and properties, if you do not follow the guidelines of ORPM you can lose it all, you know the difference between right and wrong, nobody has the right to dictate what you believe in, but if you become a problem in the system they will take your license away from you, time to start building properties that can hold a capacity of people. Stocks and bonds and Treasury can be a trap to keep you dictated, taking away your freedom of speech and belief, for instance, if you had a church, if you had a congregation of 100 to 500 to 1000 people, if you needed to shut the church down 10 to 20 or 30 houses on the Block can feel that capacity of church. Book of Philippians in the Bible, this lady had a big house, that's where church has started from, and that's where it's going to start going back to everything for a refuge, making sure that every community is well taken care of, City to City, for Block to block, from Street to Street, why be worried about a government building dealing with stocks and bonds being dictated, you must understand, pastor, the church is not about you but about a congregation about each other, nothing new underneath the sun, just like the book of Acts in the Bible, the people had a refuge, a safe place, everybody had land and property together, everybody was breaking bread and making sure everybody is taken care of. God's hand will be upon his children, there will be Refuge centers throughout the world, protection of all nationalities and races, but everywhere else will be in bondage to a New World Order. It's very important that you get to the designation zones. California; Michigan; New York; Georgia; New Orleans; Washington, D.C.; Illinois; Florida, there will be more states to go to when Revival hits the land, not to be dictated into martial law.

CHAPTER 20
Different Opinion

We have to understand the world that we live in is a spiritual World, not a physical world. So many denominations, sometimes it becomes very hard what you believe in. Pentecostal Church, Baptist Church, Seventh-Day Adventist, Jehovah's Witness, Catholic, just to name a few. I don't believe in religion but Spirituality. The world wants to keep the title religion, designed to keep confusion in the world, making the Ministries lukewarm, keeping the so-called religions divided, there's no spirituality. By not being on one accord it gives the enemy ground, some people want to worship Buddha, Confucius, Mother Mary, Muhammad, Islam, some people worship stones and trees. You have the right to believe in who you want to serve. I serve God Almighty, Jesus Christ, and the Holy Spirit, I've been used as a vessel to write this book. I've been given the wisdom and knowledge by the Holy Spirit, to understand how to put this book together. I talk about things that are mind-boggling, a vision from God to write these things down. People will call it walking in the prophetic, God allowing me to see a little bit of the future, the direction this world is going in.

Different denominations are at different levels, for instance, some people believe that Jesus Christ is not the son of God. Churches do not believe in the power of the Holy Spirit. The enemy has a strategy to keep the churches off balance, people say that the Bible has been misinterpreted. What about people saying they have found the Lost scriptures of the Bible, so how can the whole Bible be accurate and true? There's so much going on in the world today, if you do not have a true connection with God, Jesus Christ, and the Holy Spirit, you do not have anything, nothing else counts. Sure, you might say that you're not into spirituality or the whole church world scene. Look at the chain of events we're dealing with, a radical President Donald Trump, Coronavirus is in the air, people asked to wear masks, to stay in their houses, the beginning of the New World Order. Antichrist testing the waters, so if you're not praying to God Almighty to have mercy upon this world you are really confused, freedom of speech, you have the right to believe in what you want to believe in, how's it working for you, does God seem to be real to you, or are you alone being stubborn?

Trials and tribulations are just the beginning, so you need a strong Foundation, Something to Believe In. Who is your god that you serve, some people's God is sex, marijuana, alcohol, beer, cigarettes, cocaine, crystal meth, ecstasy, Sherm sticks, opium, heroin, uppers and downers. Who do you worship and bow down to, who are you chasing day in and day out to get that fix, to get that high? God, Jesus, and the Holy Spirit will keep your mind in the third heaven. There's nothing in this world that is more satisfying than Trinity. Maybe you have tried everything in the world except God Almighty and his son Jesus Christ and the Holy Spirit. God wants to take you through visions and dreams to bring manifestations in your life. On the back of a dollar bill that says In God We Trust, or do you trust the system of the government? There is a covering over the United States, God's hands upon this Earth. Foreigners have left their country to get away from Evil dictators, you have a right to choose religions, whoever you want to serve. I believe in spiritualization, my spirit living in a physical body, created to Worship father God, His Son and the Holy Spirit.

Donald Trump is a king that has been put in the White House. Is Donald Trump following the blueprints that God put into his heart, or is he making his own decisions, being diluted? God is doing a census of the USA to see who will call upon him. God Is Watching Trump very closely. God Almighty, he sees everything, he knows everything, he hears everything. Whatever you believe in is going to be tested, workers of iniquity will be Tried by the fire. Mindsets have to be for the equal Liberty, not to be overwhelmed by Life societies to live this life second-by-second, minute by minute, hour by hour. Is your foundation built on wood, clay, or brick, it makes no difference, they all can be torn down. You need all those components to be spiritual, to be successful in life, when the storms blow your house will still be standing, not a window will be busted out, not a shingle off the house, nothing but relaxation, secure in the arms of God Almighty, everybody goes through trials and tribulations, but if God has your back the way you come out of the storm will be different. Nothing will be broken, you'll come out on the other end shining.

God is the creator of the universe, all-powerful, all-knowing, magnificent in his glory. When God made Adam and Eve, I believe they were all colors, of all Nations and races, when they started having children all the nationalities became broke down. What if everybody was born with all colors, would it put an end to racism and Prejudice? We should all be equal as one, living in Harmony and peace, even though we speak different languages we bleed the same. We all cry and hurt and feel pain, you understand what it feels like to go insane. I'd rather live a positive life instead of being in negativity all the time, we all have been through sadness and depression and cried. We know what it's like to lose a loved one, we have experienced joy and happiness, we all come from the same creator. So let's learn how to live as one, there's enough land for the fellow man, we don't need to be greedy or territorial. God loves everybody the same, he's given everybody a talent, it's up to you what you do with it, bury it in the ground or Prosper off of it, that is the difference. Everybody has a chance to be successful in life, if we did not have a willpower we would be machines, but we are alive in this human body, to make a decision to believe or not to believe, different opinion.

CHAPTER 21
White America

ALL NATIONS ARE BEING TESTED BECAUSE DONALD TRUMP IS THE president of the United States. Does the name White House make a statement, is it Prejudice saying that one race rules over the other? No race should be over the next one, everybody should have an equal playing field. I'm quite sure the forefathers of this great country unanimously voted for the White House, where was the guidance for everybody else to vote for the White House, the name, if the United States was playing Fair we would not have the name the White House. The colorful house, that's a statement saying that we are one, let's talk a little bit about the forefathers who really made a statement for this country. George Washington was a liberal commander-in-chief with political power, very intelligent with combat War, a technician. George Washington kept fighting for the American people, no matter what adversity, he stood for freedom of living, freedom of speech, freedom of Rights.

Every president that was in the White House Was required to follow the DNA of the forefathers. What presidents have branched off to follow the Illuminati, is Donald Trump a part of that organization, all the former presidents that are not in office anymore, they are still a part of the big family presidents. They all have a code of honor, where they are locked into the organization. There was a government shutdown when Trump was trying to fight to get the wall built, but white Americans got a chance to look deep into Trump. White Americans are ashamed of the things that the president has been saying and doing, they feel he doesn't have the right to step on their shoes. White America feels that they are the superior race, they are not used to their own kind attacking them. Donald Trump has tried all nationalities, he doesn't mind challenging White America. Doing this he has rubbed people in power the wrong way, he has a flair for The Dramatics, that's one reason why he's in office, but for the white Americans that voted him in they see the light a different way, they understand his pattern of thinking, he has a special formula, to rule and be aggressive against the American people.

Whoever is Donald Trump Great Wall, that organization is big. The Syndicate has businesses in every city, state, country, and foreign country. Their technology is mind-blowing, I talked a little bit about the Illuminati before the powerful satellites, they have very knowledgeable about fiber-optics dealing with electricity, they can shut any city, state, or country down, very intellectual of business degrees and doctorate Degrees. Time to protect this country against people that do war crimes, making sure never again any sudden Terror in the USA. Forefathers of the USA, forefathers of the Illuminati might have different thoughts of action, about the growth and lives of the American people. Are they marching down the same road but getting different results? True reality, the struggle to be dominant between both parties approaching the New World Order, different ways. Same way with World War I and World War II, a splitting up, different people of the government look at the war in different ways, people could not see eye-to-eye, a split right in the middle or one party had more than the other. Most likely the Illuminati had more people on their side as they left a government system, if that's true they have more say-so than the government.

The forefathers of the Illuminati have been expanding the different races for some time now, if they follow their code of standards people in the USA and foreign countries have been promised protection, they have been given land and properties, well taken care of, especially when dealing with calamities, people will be able to eat good off the land. Any Necessities that they need to survive off life, as long as they have the trademark on them, High seniority for any function going on. Strong classified structural business, it has the ability at any time to capture or destroy that makes them very dangerous, just like Donald Trump if he represents Illuminati, being a hothead you cannot deny that the president is trying to put the economy in order. Trump doesn't care if you're offended or not, he has a game plan that he is set in motion. If Trump does not listen to what God wants him to do he will be judged, how can one man turn a nation upside down, why is it so much a strong hatred for this man, because he tells it like it is, some of the things that he says is right.

White America, you made your own bed hard, now you have to lie in it. Don't be so quick to get offended when Trump attacks your race. It's nothing personal but only business. He doesn't have any problem degrading you hard to the Core. Trump is giving White America a taste of their own medicine. How does it feel when you're being unfairly very rudely? White America, Prejudice has no meaning so why be afraid of what Trump is doing in the White House? Violence and hatred, it's still going on with the world today, a chip is on its shoulder. Donald Trump is not playing the race card literally, he's just a mean man, what you see from the president is what you get. Straightforward, he doesn't hide anything, he is aware of the decisions that he makes. It looks like he allows pressure to get to him, becoming irrational. That could hurt him down the long run, when he tries to become president for another 4 years. Just like playing a game of cards, don't let everybody see your hand, sometimes you have to save the best for last, instead of showing your whole hand have something to back yourself up with.

Has Donald Trump run out of steam, is his train still moving? He came out of the blocks blowing his whistle train real hard. Has he passed a lot of people Up by staying in the same gear? Could that be his downfall for being president for another 4 years, because he did not take the time to slow down, in different cities and states for the people to understand his vision? Or did he let his vindictive mouth ruin his reputation? The people that have been riding on his train since he became president, has the ride been smooth or bumpy, or has the train been delayed many times, not staying on schedule, not sticking to the script but going a different direction? Totally doing the opposite of what he told the people he would do. Did he talk a good game and tricking people into voting him in, or are the people satisfied that voted him in, do they want the train to go much faster because they feel he's not running people over fast enough, by dictating the American people missing their stop, freedom of equality, the right to be American citizens, live a normal and productive life, not going around the same Mountain but bringing change to the environment.

CHAPTER 22

Running Out of Time

EVERYBODY IS SHUT IN AND SHUT DOWN DEALING WITH THIS WHOLE Coronavirus, it has been said it is trying to affect the election coming up in November, or this is a form of retaliation against Trump's foreign countries and United States, people of higher position in the government, don't agree with Trump. Was it a tactic when they tried to impeach the president, was it designed to cool the whole world off, so people could feel good, Trump burned the world on a fire so when he was being impeached, people had a sense of relief. The system tried to gain back the minds and hearts of the American people, but it turned out to be a waste of time while CNN and different stations kept wearing out the impeachment. People had their time to get free shots in at Trump, saying how terrible he is, he will be put out of office. A whole ordeal was to stop the fire to get American people the water so they would not burn up. Donald Trump did damage to the American people, he was the Talk of the Town, to stay mad 24 hours a day, to think about Trump all the time you got it bad.

People have accused Trump of abusing his power and doing whatever he wanted to do in the White House, who hasn't in the White House abused their power? A lot of power tripping going on in the White House, everybody can be guilty of that. There's no order in the White House, everybody loves to get their point across. Supreme Court, Republicans, Democrats, everybody wants Leverage. Dictatorship to gain control while the system is failing. What is the true definition of abusing power, racial bias to be prejudiced, not to respect the constitutional rights? There was no blueprint to show how to run the White House. The president was accused of doing business deals with the Ukrainians and engaged with Russia. About being impeached, Trump was accused of being out of his mind, being very dangerous. It was said that he did not follow the guidelines, the Supreme Court wanted him to bow down to their rules. People in the White House did not like the idea of Donald Trump challenging their system.

Everybody needed Trump out of the White House, by any means necessary. The Democrats tried to push Trump out of the White House but they could not convince the Republicans. They tried to accuse him Article 1, abusing his power, Article 2, obstruction of justice misconduct. It was just a waste of time without the documents or actual Witnesses the things that the president did. They thought they had a Smoking Gun but it was cold, it was not fired, they could not accuse the president. Congress was powerless against Trump, he knew it. When he was being impeached he stood up with a boldness, he knew he wasn't going anywhere. His Showmanship of arrogance was very nerve-wracking to the American people, as he stood there in oath, people despised him, he made people sick to their stomachs. He got a kick out of making people mad, making an impact in the world, truly he was winning.

You have a right to freedom of speech, to believe in what you want to. True patriotism, the American way, we would not want it any other way. Judging people for wrong reasons, you're not adding to Life Society but you are bringing on a sense of disbelief. Regardless if you fought for this great land or work hard in this great land, don't judge people's patriotism, there's so many people that are heroes in the world, John F. Kennedy, Martin Luther King, Barack Obama, George Washington, men that have paved their way through the world. Is Donald Trump one of these men that has stood for something to bring about change in this world? So why try to manipulate somebody to keep them in bondage and in Chains if he hasn't done anything, the old system of this world is not working, it's time for a new change, so if Trump is bringing this why accuse him? The American people are tired of being in Chains, freedom of democracy.

Trump came into the White House to tear down division of walls, rebuild the foundation to make sure the structural of walls are right, to make sure the American people are living freely, freedom of Liberty, to make sure everybody has a safe playing field, that the welfare of the American people have a balance, owning land and properties, to make sure that the American people are not being cheated by a corrupt government system. All nationalities and all Races should have the right to strive for equality, there should not be One race that has more than the other. All nationalities have worked hard on the soil, everybody should have the same playing field. There should not be any favoritism, fair is fair, you deserve everything like the next man does, especially if you have put in the time and effort, you have the right to be kings and queens like everybody else, you should have the best and everything that life has to offer you. There's no way that you should settle for less, if you deserve it it needs to be rewarded to you.

The American dream doesn't mean anything if you can't share it with your loved ones. You don't know the meaning of life, all you see is poverty and hatred, the decisions of your father and mother to live life unproductively, you become a picture of Life Society. Donald Trump was raised with the Finer Things in life, so he understated how to live life to the fullest. He wants to make sure that all the American people have the tools for success. Make sure that the economy is booming, there's enough jobs for the American people, having medical and dental, able to get transportation, everything to make it in life. Unfortunately some people don't understand what it means to be homeless, not to have food in your stomach. I wouldn't wish that on no one, but the world that we live in today it's a part of life. Donald Trump does not wish that the American people will suffer, in poverty like a lot of foreign countries, do they don't care about their people? They have the best of everything in life, while their people suffer. Very Sinister and bold to see third-world countries suffering with the little children. Donald Trump might seem to be mean and outrageous but he is not that cruel to see humans suffer like they do over in foreign countries. I know that Donald Trump wants to accomplish a lot of things, is he running out of time? Or will he have another four years to get everything out of his system? The Nations believe that Trump would be president for another 4 years. Stop Running Scared, we have faced the Coronavirus, we can make it through anything. If it has been designed by God for Trump to be president for another 4 years, Embrace change.

CHAPTER 23
Containment

Still dealing with the Coronavirus, today is May 3rd, 2020. I went outside to get a break from staying indoors. I decided to go to the Dollar Tree to look for a dollar movie or $5 movie. I stumbled across the movie called *Containment*, release of 2015 by Vision Films, neighbors staying in a complex apartment waking up in the morning, doors and windows sealed shut. Strangers in hazmat suits infiltrate the apartments, taking residence. While they infected the building with the virus they had no water or electricity. There was no way to leave the apartment. There Was Fear everywhere, people were having nervous breakdowns and we're panicking in the apartments. Something like the Coronavirus, manmade to test the population, people trapped in their own apartment as they tried to get out. Underneath their door, what's this white glue-ish substances that had the door sealed in, they could not get out. People tried to use their cell phones, to their amazement they didn't have a signal. Also it was hot that day, people did not have a fan or air conditioner, they were left to die.

People started banging on the windows at these people in orange suits, they had tents set up outside, caution areas saying contamination, keep on your mask and gloves, the residents had their backs put to the wall so they started busting through the walls of the apartments. They started going from unit to unit, people started drilling their way out of the apartments. The neighbors got their weapons and guns and rallied together, they took a stand against the people in the orange suits with a mask. They were able to take one hostage, and ask him what was happening. A virus was released throughout the apartment to reach the population in 24 hours. Virus designed to attack old people, first the middle-aged and then the Young, neighbors found an antidote on the people with the orange suits and masks. It was for the children as they were doing a study on them. Everybody in the complex was infected. They had no chance of survival but the children did, the rest of the people were used as guinea pigs.

When the other neighbors had heard that there was an antidote, everybody went to the apartment to try to break in but they would not turn over the guy in the orange suit or the antidote, so they tried to break into the doors, anything they can find, they were now fighting against each other. They demanded the antidote, it was now 50 against 5, escaping through the holes in the walls that they created in the apartments. Eventually they got some of the people along with the person in the orange suit, but he no longer had the antidote. The guy that captured him, he took off with the antidote and took it for himself while he was shot down. As the people were going berserk in the apartments, the building was very tall, the people in the orange suits outside with the mask and gloves on put a chemical through the air vent, it would knock the people unconscious. So as the smoke came through the vents, people really started to panic. One guy and a little boy and an old lady escape to get on top of the roof of the high-rise, getting away from the chemical that they put through the vent system.

As they made it to the top of the roof, everybody was exhausted and fearful for their life. When they woke in the morning the old lady had passed, she escaped the chemicals put through the vent, but she could not escape the virus because she was infected already, the guy that has survived with the little boy, he was on his way out, the virus was getting to him. They made it out, he told the little boy to keep his eyes shut while he put him on his back. There were so many bodies around because of the virus as he made it outside, he told the little boy to get away. As the boy was walking he was sad and all alone, somebody approached him from the back, it was one of the people in the orange suit, taken to a building with children 7 to 12 years old, as they did experiments on them with the antidote telling them everything will be fine.

The movie really hit home to me, thank God that we were not trapped in our homes and apartments. Not able to breathe without electricity or water, it has not been that extreme, but to some people's standards to be afflicted with this virus manmade, it definitely hasn't been Godly, nothing but sad and pitiful, all the lives we lost due to this virus. The restrictions that have been put on the American people, the collapse of the economy through restaurants, people with businesses losing money, people not able to pay their mortgage or rent, car notes, you name it. People should be held accountable for releasing this virus, did Trump know about it ahead of time? People do not know but one thing I do know, just like in that movie the little kids should not have to suffer. To use weapons of mass destruction, it's a sin, a virus like this that affected the whole world, that's crazy, people have really been tried in their minds, not able to rest and relax, staying on the edge, ready to crumble at any given time. Everything totally has been turned upside down, 2020, it's something to be reckoned with, man has become evil to the Core. I wonder what disasters are heading our way without a heads-up. I know that life is not fair sometimes but this time it's off the chain.

Through this whole ordeal, God is the only one that we can trust to keep praying to keep the faith this will soon end. What a world we live in, everybody is anxiously ready to get back to life, but truly did you learn something, not to take life for granted. Always give a helping hand to your fellow man, don't steal, cheat, or kill, stop being mean, rude, obnoxious. The bottom line is the world needs love, everybody has had a chance to display love. I know Times Like These are hard but if we hold on we can grow stronger. There's nothing wrong with telling people that you're sorry, there's nothing wrong with telling people that you will try to get better. Keep fighting and put in the effort to defeat the Coronavirus, that it will not wipe out the whole population. Social distancing, keeping our hands washed, covering our mouth has been very important, a technique designed to slow down the virus, to make it lose its strength. Slowly but surely we will get back to life, time to make our surroundings better. As American people we need to learn how to stay more on guard, aware of our circumstances, ready to face any crisis we deal with, praying to God Almighty will give us a strong Foundation to make it through anything. Don't let the cares of the world get you down, you are a strong Survivor and a conqueror.

CHAPTER 24
Out of Mind

IT'S VERY IMPORTANT THAT WE STAY IN OUR RIGHT MIND THROUGH LIFE'S trials, we all are facing our greatest fear, we have to keep our minds renewed. If you keep a journal or system of everyday living you release the stress. You have to understand the spiritual world we live in, not a physical but the mental strain of day-in-day-out situations. People like to work out or jog, whatever it takes to release the stress, everybody has been ordered to stay shut in, practice social distancing. People are not used to being confined indoors, they said it feels like jail. Confusion is in the air, Americans still can't wrap their minds around the Coronavirus. There has to be a mechanism in order to shut down fear and worry, praying it's helpful, laughter can ease the mind, playing board games, or basketball, baseball, football, Xbox games, find a way to take out the focus of uncertain times we live in.

Everybody deals with stress differently, I wonder, how does the president deal with stress? A lot of people saying that the president is happy to see the world suffering, I know that the president does not wish the Coronavirus on anyone, he cannot be that insane, but the president over there in China is a basket case, he should be tried for espionage. Does he have that much power to still walk around free and accusing Americans that it came from us? I guess the whole human race is nothing but guinea pigs used for experimentation, told to stay indoors. President Trump, you should shut down all activities that we have with China in the USA. Governments are working with governments and also foreign countries to create antidotes. China and other foreign countries, if you know of a vaccine get it to the human race, no more games, the lives are piling up due to the Virus, this is what's making the world crazy.

A lot of people that own businesses have really felt the sting of Covid-19, business owners never thought in their right minds that they would face a dilemma like this. For the first time a lot of owners have experienced filing for unemployment, dealing with a state of emergency, a lot of businesses were already behind, now they are fearful of shutting down for good. Retirement funds have Been spent up, mortgages on people's house, stocks and bonds, you name it. People have to reset their budgets, cut down on the activities going from Rich class to middle class from middle-class to poor class. When will the nightmare be over? I was on my way to the bank, going to the teller machine, it had to be at least 12 to 15 teenagers together smoking weed and drinking beer right in public, standing in the middle of the street, daring someone to hit them, as the light turned green for the cars to go. With the schools being closed everybody's Reckless, and this was 9 in the morning, walking around, looking at people crazy. I have a 10-year-old daughter and she's all over the place while she has to stay home, if you think it was a handful before the Coronavirus hit, with our children, it's really hard trying to slow them down for them to listen.

To fight an unseen battle is very time consuming because you never know when the Coronavirus will strike. It builds from surface-to-surface, whatever way it can spread it will. That's why it's very important to wash your hands. Keep your nose and your mouth covered. Practice social distancing. I take my hat off to the people working in the hospitals that have to deal upfront with patients. You have to be really strong and pray that you will not catch the virus. 14 days to discover the symptoms or 14 days after the symptoms, I've heard different sayings from people, I'm taking everything and putting it into consideration. We truly do not know if the Coronavirus will come back in the future, it's a possibility, man should not have the capability of releasing viruses, just like American soldiers coming home dealing with post syndrome. Coronavirus is a war chemical, one of the many chemicals Russia and China possesses.

A lot of people are mad at God Almighty, saying how could he let this happen. Even ministers are mad, saying what happened to God's mercy and Grace. Remember that the Coronavirus was manmade, God is not in the business of putting out viruses. All he has to do is snap his fingers and you're gone in the Wind. Man has gotten beside himself, too much power for his own sense. God will sit back and see the destruction of man, yes, God does hear the prayers of the righteous, right now he is separating the wheat from the tear, everything has gotten entwined together, you don't know who's coming or going, who's good or bad, believe me, God has his foot on this Earth, if he didn't man would have destroyed this Earth a long time ago. It's a Dreadful thing to fall into the arms of Almighty God , whoever released this Coronavirus, God is watching, he has your number. Believe me, you reap what you sow, how's your conscience doing when you go to sleep at night, knowing that you have affected the whole world?

This book will go down in history as one of the best, it is a blueprint for the Next Generation. Right now it will come in handy for Our Generation, the year 2020. When we think back down the line four or five years from now, how the year 2020 sucker punched us in our mouths, everybody will have that scar branded on our backs, a permanent tattoo that can never be removed. Things were already bad enough, the whole world was in shock, Kobe Bryant and his daughter passed away and the rest of the people aboard the helicopter. Very painful to hear and still is, now we're fighting face to face with the boogeyman Coronavirus. Its mission is to destroy civilization, to take away life, to watch people suffer. Storms of life have been very hard since Trump has become president, I'm not saying that he is toxic, would the world agree that he should not become president again because trouble and Mischief follows him? He really knows how to crash a party, swell guy with a big heart, unorthodox style of play, extraordinary one of a kind that doesn't come around often. Something that has been in the making for years, now that he has evolved will it be hard to get rid of him? Or do you want more of him, we will find out with the elections coming up in November.

CLOSING

IN CLOSING THIS BOOK, THE JOURNEY HAS BEEN LONG. I have been really educated by the Holy Spirit while writing *Trump Has Blown*. I have had to have patience in watching the process of this book unfold right in front of my eyes. What a revelation of the direction the USA is hitting in. I've come a long way in writing this book, when I first started writing this book the election was going on with Trump and Clinton, at that time I had no Direction, no Foundation on what the book was truly about. I had to put my trust in faith in God because I have been a vessel that has been used to put this book out through the Holy Spirit. At times when writing the book I would be happy, sad, mad, confused, and in disarray with my emotions, not knowing how to feel. I would go to sleep at times very distracted, very emotional and very encouraged when the Holy Spirit showed me that his hand is upon the United States. There is hope, faith is the substance of things believe in but not seen, so I stopped leaning on my own understanding and put my trust in faith in Almighty God because I was a vessel used by him to bring the anointing out to this book. When reading this book you need to have an open mind through the Holy Spirit. I can't believe how time is flying. Trump's time is almost up in the White House, and he's trying to win the elections again, four years is almost went by, that's the beauty of these books. God gives me every single book that he's allowed me to write. God has a certain time and season that he wants me to release these books. In closing, may God keep you in his perfect peace.

GEORGE FLOYD

THE WHOLE WORLD HAS BEEN TURNED UPSIDE DOWN BEHIND THE brutal killing of George Floyd, protesting is everywhere, people are starting to take a stand against police Injustice. It definitely was a tragedy to see the death of this man on TV, how they show the police officer with his knee on the neck of George Floyd while he shouted out, "I cannot breathe." The police officer deliberately knew what he was doing, right along with his accomplice, it was spontaneous and very calculated to see a human being suffering like that, would make anybody mad, nobody deserves to die like that. Just like I talked about in the chapter "Community Clean-up" and the resistance all Races are now protesting, black Americans, white Americans, Indian-Americans, Mexican-Americans, Asian-Americans, Ethiopian-Americans, the reason why I say American all nations are in this country. Injustice of police officers has been going on for centuries, this is nothing new Underneath the Sun, but the George Floyd killings has sparked a revolution, the whole world has been woken, everybody truly sees the light but will it make a difference or will the world continue to be dark and have no remorse for minorities?

It hurts my heart to see the turmoil and the struggles minorities have been through, the last words that came out of George Floyd's mouth was "Mama," his last breath. We have to understand that there is a spirit of Prejudice and hatred for minorities, people being shot down by police officers who think that they are above the law. They think that there's no penalty for their actions, that's why they've been getting away with it for centuries because they hide behind a badge to think that they are gods. How can we feel safe, the police officers are here to protect and serve, not to destroy and kill, truly this world system has failed us. I truly hope and pray that George Floyd's death will not be in vain, that the American people understand we bleed the same. We all have loved ones, what if it was your loved ones that suffered a terrible death, every time I think about George Floyd what he went through I cannot hold back the tears, the pain that I feel will continue to burn inside me until there is truly a resolution in the world we live in. I know that this anger, this fire has to be put out inside my soul, because if not there will be a destructive spirit that will continue to have an outrage that all nations and races are feeling in the United States, to want to destroy anything that is in their pathway.

The destructive Behavior that's been going on throughout United States has been very tremendous, anger, resentment, a buildup, it's been in the making for years, people have been fed up, tired of seeing Injustices of hate crimes swept under the rug, where the system has let people go free, knowing that the crime they committed they should have been found guilty. Now there's a backlash, the year 2020, the resistance, the right to take a stand for equal rights. George Floyd has become a pioneer, a catalyst, a martyr that represents stop the injustice, he truly has paved the way for the millions of Souls destroyed through police brutality. Why did it have to take such a brutal approach, the way this man suffered to gain recognition throughout the whole world, the whole world was already on the edge dealing with the Coronavirus, commanded to stay indoors, social distancing, people were already frustrated, feel like they were stuck behind bars, waiting to get back to their everyday life routine, tired of the restrictions, being forced to do something they don't want to do by the government as the Coronavirus is still going Buck Wild. The timing of George Floyd's death truly set the American people over the edge. There is a Changing of the Guard, we truly have got a chance to see the different nationalities in the United States that truly understand we bleed the same that has taken a stand for our fellow man, understanding that racism is wrong.

Being from Minneapolis, Minnesota, I have had a chance to see things boil over, driving through the city I have seen the destructive Behavior of the American people, tired of the system not having rules put in place for police officers or Sheriffs to let them know they will suffer repercussions if they committed crimes, they should be prosecuted like the next person, even though the hatred, the hurt, the discomfort to watch a helpless man at the mercy of a police officer being suffocated over 8 minutes and some seconds with his knees on George Floyd's neck. For the whole world to see it was unbearable. People began to Light the City of Minneapolis and St. Paul on fire, destroying people's businesses. All the stores that I used to go to burned to the ground, Cubs Food Store, Target, Kmart, Wendy's, AutoZone, Wells Fargo, US Bank, pawn shops, dollar stores, Walgreens, people were going into store stealing clothes, shoes, taking food out of the grocery stores, it was total chaos, burning down police stations, Domino's, liquor stores, Speedway gas stations, Holiday gas stations, USA post office, gas stations, buildings being spray-painted, Popeyes. Subway, Aldi's food store, Planet Fitness.

It was so bad the National Guard had to come out to shut the city down, the City of Minneapolis and St. Paul went into a state of emergency, everything was boarded up, all the businesses, there was a curfew, people had to be in by 8 at night, gas stations were closed, the question was asked, why where people looting and destroying things? What did George Floyd's death have to do with the destruction of their property? The answer was that the buildings that they occupied were owned by the government the system that let the American people down, so they wanted to send a strong message to let the government know that if they want to beat up and kill minorities that they would destroy the Government properties and beat up on the buildings, not knowing that everybody would suffer behind this. The people that did not cause any harm or damage to their properties, now in order to go to the grocery store it's hard to get food because there's no business downtown, the grocery stores are way far out, the ones that have not been destroyed. So the poor, the middle class is really struggling to keep food on the table, a lot of businesses still have their properties boarded up, scared to open up for business because they don't know if the people are done retaliating. All throughout the city, the professional art drawers have drawn pictures of George Floyd, a lot of the pictures are very colorful, every time I see George Floyd's face on a wall or a building I am moved to tears. I know that he is in the Kingdom of Heaven, a joint Heir with Christ, seated in Heavenly places. My condolences go out to his family, even though he's not on this Earth with us but his spirit is present in the hearts and minds and Souls of the American people, long live the momentum of George Floyd. He definitely will make a difference for the year 2020. His life Legacy will always be remembered, little children will be talking about him when they become of old age, something to pass down to their children generations to Generations. I know that somebody somewhere is making t-shirts in his honor. I truly hope that President Donald Trump will repent for his actions, the things that he said about the National Guard going to the different cities and states to Forge war if they have to, there's a better solution to the madness, right now the whole world needs hope to get through the Coronavirus and George Floyd because people are still dying to an evil system of police brutality.